GRACE-*full*
LEADERSHIP

GRACE-*full*
LEADERSHIP

understanding the heart
of a Christian leader

John C. Bowling

BEACON HILL PRESS
OF KANSAS CITY

Copyright 2000, 2011
by Beacon Hill Press of Kansas City

First edition 2000
Second edition 2011

ISBN 978-0-8341-2602-2

Printed in the
United States of America

Cover Design: Arthur Cherry
Interior Design: Sharon Page

Library of Congress Cataloging-in-Publication Data

Bowling, John C., 1949-
    Grace-full leadership : understanding the heart of a christian leader / John C. Bowling. — 2nd ed.
        p. cm.
    Includes bibliographical references.
    ISBN 978-0-8341-2602-2 (hardcover)
    1. Christian leadership. I. Title.
    BV652.1.B69 2011
    253—dc22

                                                            2010051632

10 9 8 7 6 5 4 3 2 1

DEDICATION

This book is respectfully dedicated to Vernon Bowling, my father, and John Cheeseman, my father-in-law, two grace-full leaders who built outstanding businesses while honoring God as much on Monday as they did on Sunday.

*Everyone has an obligation
as well as the privilege of
leading in something.*

—Charles E. Jones

CONTENTS

ABOUT THE AUTHOR

John Bowling has served as president of Olivet Nazarene University since 1991 and is the author of *A Way with Words* (Beacon Hill Press of Kansas City, 1999). Bowling is a former pastor and professor, and he continues to be active in a variety of professional organizations and the local community. He currently serves on the Board of Directors for Rush Presbyterian/St. Luke's Hospital and University in Chicago, the Bradley-Bourbonnais Area Chamber of Commerce, First of America Bank, and the Riverside Medical Center Board. As a church leader, Dr. Bowling also serves on the International General Board of the Church of the Nazarene, the Board of Directors of the Nazarene Publishing House in Kansas City, and the USA Canada Council of Education and International Board of Education for the Church of the Nazarene.

He and his wife, Jill, reside in Bourbonnais, Illinois.

FOREWORD

The stunning and magnificent new Betty and Kenneth Hawkins Centennial Chapel was recently completed on the campus of Olivet Nazarene University. This 3,046-seat chapel was built at a cost of about $25 million dollars. Instead of making payments on a mortgage for years to come, President John Bowling made the decision to go out and raise the money. The entire amount! The goal was accomplished and there is no mortgage to pay. I will listen to a leader like that.

Several years ago, this 50-something university president flew thousands of miles away from his home in Bourbonnais, Illinois, to the African nation of Tanzania to join a mountain climbing team. We are not talking Pike's Peak here—we are talking the 19,341-foot mountain named Kilimanjaro. Another book was born in the heart and mind of this university president on that never-to-be-forgotten climb, *Making the Climb*. John Bowling didn't read about mountain climbing—he experienced it. His story will take your breath away. I will listen to a leader like that.

Everyone knows that National Football League teams are a rough-and-tumble bunch. The stories of their on-and-off field escapades are legendary. To the amazement of all, one such team—the Chicago Bears—approached this university president with a request to use the campus of Olivet Nazarene University as the location for their annual one-month preseason training camp. John Bowling entertained the idea and then calmly but firmly said, "This is a no-drug, no-alcohol, no-tobacco campus. Will the Chicago Bears be willing to honor these Christian convictions?" The answer was yes! The Bears have now come to the campus of O.N.U. for years, four weeks at a time; the public has come to watch their beloved Bears by the thousands; and it still is a "no-drug, no-alcohol, no-tobacco campus." How could John Bowling pull that one off? I don't know—but I will listen to a leader like that.

A few months ago I was privileged to speak at the fall revival services at Olivet Nazarene University. I haven't seen anything like what happened there in ten years or more! Overflow evening crowds of one thousand plus, chairs in the aisles and foyer, at the close of every message young adults (plus teens, senior adults, and ages in between) were kneeling all across the front of the sanctuary seeking God's grace, God's will, and God's transforming power in their lives. As one person said, "God was all over the place!" In the midst of that scene of people kneeling, praying, and seeking God, I saw President John Bowling kneeling with his arms around several college students, praying for God's peace to come to their troubled hearts. He was not on the platform watching; he was among these young adults praying and giving godly counsel. Again, I saw personal, Spirit-filled leadership in action. I will listen to a leader like that!

This wise and godly man has opened his heart and mind to us in his book *Grace-Full Leadership*. Read it to your soul's delight. In the words of Dr. Bowling, This isn't a book "on the *how* of leadership . . . but more the *who* of leadership, the *ends* of leadership, and the *environment* of leadership." As you read these pages you will soon agree with me, "We will listen to, follow, and learn from a leader like that!"

—James H. Diehl
General Superintendent Emeritus

INTRODUCTION

An Overview of Grace-Full Leadership

The subtitle of this book, *Understanding the Heart of a Christian Leader,* carries with it certain assumptions.

1. *The phrase implies that leadership within the context and life of the Christian community is, or at least ought to be, different from other kinds of leadership.*

The ways of business, military, or governmental leadership should not necessarily be the leadership ways of the Christian leader. Secular methods of management need not always be the model for men and women whose hearts have been impacted by the grace of God.

Moral relativism, a bottom-line mentality, an insensitivity to social responsibility, and an abuse of power too often characterize general leadership. Jesus indicated a different approach to leadership. This is seen in one of His discourses with the disciples.

"Jesus called [his disciples] together and said, 'You know that those who are regarded as rulers of the Gentiles lord it over them, and their high officials exercise authority over them. Not so with you. Instead, whoever wants to become great among you must be your servant, and whoever wants to be first must be slave of all'" (Mark 10:42-44).

Consider the dynamic tensions at work here—the tension between servanthood and leadership, for example. "Whoever wants to become great among you must be your servant, and whoever wants to be first must be slave of all," Jesus said (Mark 10:43-44). What a paradox this poses! "Leadership and servanthood are biblical concepts in creative tension—neither one can be exploited, neither can be denied."[1]

I believe that this stress is resolved only through the grace of God, His hand at work in daily life. Mediating this and other tensions enables a Christian leader to be tough-minded and tenderhearted, driven and patient, focused on task and yet attentive to others.

Not only does this passage from the Gospel of Mark turn on the word "instead," but also the whole leadership philosophy of Christ rests in these verses. Notice the contrasts—"servant[s]" instead of "high officials," and "slave of all" instead of those who "exercise authority over them." These words of Jesus reveal that there are leadership qualities and practices that are distinct within the Christian community.

2. *The subtitle implies that leadership can be understood.*

That's no small implication. While it may be true that leadership can be understood, doing so is not automatic and certainly not easy. There are no "Ten Easy Steps to Becoming a Leader," no shortcuts, no overnight successes, no fast-food formulas to produce "McLeaders." Leadership is more complex and dynamic than the easy definitions seem to imply.

James MacGregor Burns, in his Pulitzer prize-winning volume, *Leadership,* suggests that leadership is one of the most observed and yet least understood phenomena on earth.[2]

While he may be right, the quest to understand leadership is certainly widespread. Anyone who reviews the available literature or simply walks through a bookstore will note the volumes of material that seek to unravel the mysteries of leading effectively. The shelves are filled with metaphors, allegories, narratives, and case studies seeking to help readers gain a better understanding of what it means and what it takes to be a leader.

With each new book comes added pressure on the next writer to find a hook, an engaging angle or perspective from which to write. The best example of this may be the 1999 publication by Rhonda Abrams titled *Wear Clean Underwear: Business Wisdom from Mom.*[3]

Despite its wacky title, this book has merit. Abrams takes 13 homespun lessons and translates that advice into the world of work. Her chapter titles include:

- I Don't Care Who Made This Mess, Just Clean It Up
- How Do You Know You Don't Like It When You Have Never Tried It?
- If All Your Friends Jumped Off a Bridge, Would You Jump Too?
- If You Keep Making That Face, Someday It Will Freeze That Way
- Don't Get Too Big for Your Britches
- Say You're Sorry
- It's Not the End of the World
- Quit Picking on Each Other
- Share

Although leadership is a wide field of study with implications as varied as every leader and every leadership context, it can be understood, at least in part. And surely any person in such a role must strive to become the best leader possible.

3. *The subtitle suggests that the narrative represents an understanding, rather than the understanding, of Christian leadership.*

The purpose of this volume is to stir your thinking and set forth an understanding of leadership, which I've titled *Grace-Full Leadership.* I am not thinking of graceful, but grace-full—that is, grace-filled leadership. The focus is not so much on the *how* of leadership (do this and this and you will be a great leader), but more the *who* of leadership, the *ends* of leadership, and the *environment* of leadership.

Like many others, I live and work within a matrix of leadership. To a large degree, my task is to lead other leaders. I find myself regularly engaged with academic leaders, student leaders, and university trustees. I interface with a group of denominational leaders; with my colleagues at other schools, colleges, and universities; with hundreds of pastors; and with the strong and dedicated men and women who serve on various boards and committees.

In such an environment, the eternal measure of the quality and effectiveness of leadership depends upon one's willingness and ability to become a grace-filled leader. Christian leadership is fundamentally different from all other leadership. Even if the organization looks like a secular organization, there is still a difference—for God's Spirit is at work in the heart, life, and leadership of a grace-full person.

Through God's grace, leaders are transformed from the inside out. This change of heart results in the manifestation of certain Christlike qualities and traits that become the hallmarks, benchmarks, and trademarks of grace-full leadership.

— SECTION ONE —

The Qualities of Grace-Full Leadership

Grace-full leaders . . .

- ◆ are more concerned with spirit than style
- ◆ are covenantal rather than contractual
- ◆ view people as ends—not means
- ◆ recognize the changeable from the changeless
- ◆ seek significance, not just success
- ◆ are responsive as well as responsible
- ◆ are high-touch
- ◆ maximize influence and minimize authority
- ◆ are passionate
- ◆ focus primarily on the body, not the head

Leadership is both something you are and something you do.
—Fred Smith

Your attitude should be the same as that of Christ Jesus.
—Phil. 2:5

1

GRACE-*full* LEADERS . . .
are more concerned with spirit than style

No two leaders are alike. Leadership takes many forms and varies naturally from situation to situation and person to person. Leaders have different management philosophies and personality traits. Some leaders are logical and methodical, others are emotional and impulsive. Although there is no one formula for effective leadership, there are certain qualities that transform how people view leadership. A grace-full leader is one whose primary concern is not style but spirit.

Leadership style varies with personality and context. A person who seems controlling in one situation might appear an equal participant in another situation. Another may lead by the sheer force of personality under some circumstances but through careful process when the circumstances are different. Christian leaders should not try to homogenize their leadership styles. In fact, there are obvious times in the life of organizations when individuals should boldly break out of the pack and lead. But those break-out leaders must be grace-filled leaders, not ego-filled.

If an individual is to be a grace-full leader, God must be rightly placed at the center of his or her life, work, and relationships. The grace of God at work in those dimensions produces a leadership difference—not a difference of style but of spirit.

It's popular today to concentrate on the rationale side of leadership, on getting things done in the "right" way. This preoccupation with style makes it all too easy to overlook the powerful untapped source of energy and motivation coming from a proper spirit. Reason *can't* solve all problems.

Understanding leadership begins with attention to who we are and not just what we do. While it is appropriate for managers to evaluate their leadership styles from time to time, all leaders must recognize that "as practice is to policy, so style is to belief. Style is merely a consequence of what we believe, of what is in our hearts."[1]

Leadership is the tapestry of integrity
of heart and life, words and deeds,
thoughts and actions.

Leading from the inside out is an expression of grace-full leadership. A grace-full leader has the right combination of confidence and humility to recognize strengths and weaknesses and to consciously seek to build character, competency, and the confidence of those who are led. This formula is a key component of leadership.

Leadership is intensely personal and public at the same time. "It's just impossible to be a closet leader."[2] Because of the public nature of leadership, leaders are often held to a higher standard. Thus, a leader must be an example of honesty and dependability. Leadership is the tapestry of integrity of heart and life, words and deeds, thoughts and actions.

Living with integrity means wholeness, completeness, and consistency. The Scripture notes: "The integrity of the upright guides them, but the unfaithful are destroyed by their duplicity" (Prov. 11:3). Being a person of integrity is essential for anyone in leadership, and the expression of integrity is a function of spirit more than style. Like leadership itself, integrity is something you are, not something you do.

All of this means that a Christian's understanding of leadership must be theological as well as technical, for beliefs and being precede doing. Our values must be as closely integrated into our working life as they are into our family and church life. For example, if we believe that each person is made in the image of God, then for those of us who have received the gift of leadership from the people we lead, this belief has enormous implications.

Such a belief transforms how leaders view the people with whom and for whom they work. We come to value and respect others apart from what they do or how well they do it. We broaden our mission from simply managing results to leading and developing people. This shift grows in us a spirit of service. In his book *Not by Bread Alone,* Bryant Hinckley writes:

> Service is the virtue that distinguished the great of all times and which they will be remembered by. It places a mark of nobility upon its disciples. It is the dividing line which separates the two great groups of the world—those who help and those who hinder, those who lift and those who lean, those who contribute and those who only consume. How much better it is to give than to receive. Service in any form is comely and beautiful. To give encourage-

ment, to impart sympathy, to show interest, to banish fear, to build self-confidence and awaken hope in the hearts of others, in short—to love them and to show it—is to render the most precious service.[3]

Such a shift in spirit will inform and enrich our leadership style in any given situation, for the truth is, people want to be led, not managed. A leader with the right spirit knows that individuals, regardless of their position in the hierarchy, have the same basic set of needs, rights, and expectations as he or she.

A leader with the right style may be able to get people to do what needs to be done, but the grace-full leader whose focus is on spirit as well as style can motivate people to *want* to do what needs to be done. The difference in organizational culture is enormous.

When we focus simply on leadership style, we find ourselves concentrating on the wrong things:

- the bottom line rather than the horizon
- mistakes rather than possibilities
- control rather than confidence
- reputation rather than relationships

When we recognize that there is more to leadership than style, the focus shifts from method to spirit. We:

- coach rather than control
- mentor as well as manage
- strengthen others, not just supervise their work
- empower, not just employ
- create shared visions

Style and spirit are both important. But without spirit, even a good leadership style is sterile. It may produce some short-term results, but it is powerless to transform an organization into a living organism.

Grace-full leaders recognize and accept that they are stewards of trust—that they are interdependent and responsible to others. Such a leader knows that a person's rights are much less important than a person's obligations.

Grace-full leadership brings into view something different than the styles so prevalent in leadership literature. Focusing on spirit rather than style strengthens the concept that the leader is not preoccupied with conformity for conformity's sake but rather creating a vision-centered environment where objectives and expectations are met through the efforts of individuals who don't just *work* for the company but *are* the company.

The real power and energy of grace-full leaders rests in the relationship of both the leader and the followers to a commonly held set of values and objectives instead of merely the relationship of the leader to the follower.

○━━◆━━○

A focus on spirit more than style implies
that leadership must be value-centered.

○━━◆━━○

At the opening of a new school year at our university not long ago, I spoke at length with our faculty and staff about the difference between being a Christian university and a university of Christians. We cannot be as a whole what we are not as individuals. It is vital that everyone on our faculty and staff is a person of faith. To the extent that we are not what God calls us to be as individuals, who we are as a university is diminished.

A focus on spirit more than style implies that leadership must be value-centered. Leaders strive to engage the entire organization in a process of values clarification. That is a two-sided coin. First, leaders must guide the organization toward determining by what values it will operate. "What should our values be? Where are we in conflict over these issues?" Second, leaders must also determine what values are currently in place in the organization. The reality of the values in place might be disappointingly distant from the organization's mission statement.

When the values of an organization are clearly articulated, they must be effectively communicated both internally and externally. You can do this in several ways: through routine communications, by way of special events that focus on company values, and by the public recognition of individuals who model those expectations.

Leaders must also find ways to monitor how well the values are being embraced and communicated. Do the formal reporting systems deal only with bottom-line issues? Is recognition given only to those who meet their quota, no matter what?

Decisions made throughout the organization must harmonize with core values, and this emphasis should be a continuous concern. It can't be "We're doing values this year, last year it was market share, and next year it will be 'total quality management.'" Clear and consistent values are a vital part of grace-full leadership.

Closely aligned with an emphasis on values is the recognition that leadership is character in action. Character is not a function or product of style. The word comes from the idea of engraving. My father was a printer who became a publisher. When I was a young boy, he was the production manager of the daily newspaper in our county seat. In my visits to him at work I learned that in the printing business each letter is called a character. The idea is that each letter leaves a distinctive mark. Just so, a leader's character is defined by the mark he or she leaves behind. Character is the sum of a person's values, actions, and attitudes. For the leader, character resides not in one's style but in one's spirit, and the right leadership spirit is a product of the heart. From the heart flows moral courage, conviction, and conscience as well as compassion.

If you once forfeit the confidence of your fellow citizens,
you can never regain their respect and esteem.
—Abraham Lincoln

He has made us competent as ministers of a new covenant—
not of the letter but of the Spirit; for the letter kills, but the Spirit gives life.
—2 Cor. 3:6

2

GRACE-*full* LEADERS . . .

are covenantal rather than contractual

Too often leadership is seen only in contractual terms. The contractual relationship covers the quid pro quo of working together—expectations, compensation, and other such things. Contracts or other forms of expectations such as job descriptions are a normal and necessary part of the workplace, but more important in the life of any Christian leader should be the covenantal relationship.

Max DePree makes an interesting observation in his classic book *Leadership Is an Art.* He writes: "The best people working for organizations are like volunteers. Since they could probably find good jobs in any number of groups, they choose to work somewhere for reasons less tangible than salary or position. Volunteers do not need contracts, they need covenants."[1]

People need to belong not just legally but also spiritually. I believe the grace of God can enable leaders to create covenantal communities, and through that covenantal synergy accomplish more for the organization as well as the kingdom of God.

As a university president, this means that although there is a contract between the faculty or staff member and the university, I must move that relationship beyond the contract to a covenantal relationship that induces freedom and transforms the relationship between us from employer/employee to colleagues.

Grace-full leaders have a way of simply expecting the best from the people around them. They know that people can and do change and grow and learn from mistakes and successes. A covenantal relationship creates an environment for this kind of growth and development because your worth is not governed solely by the letter of the law or the bottom line.

Grace-full leadership understands that enabling others to reach their potential is, in a way, a mysterious thing. It can't be forced or manipulated; it must be allowed to take root, to grow, and finally to blossom naturally.

It is important for any leader to recognize that any accomplishment takes teamwork. In a way, it is the follower who ultimately determines the success or failure of the leader. Thus, the goals of the organization are best met when the goals and needs of the people in the organization are met.

Aleksandr Solzhenitsyn, in his celebrated speech to the 1978 graduating class of Harvard College, noted:

A society based on the letter of the law and never reaching any higher fails to take advantage of the full range of human possibilities. The letter of the law is too cold and formal to have a beneficial influence on society. Whenever the tissue of life is woven of legalistic relationships, this creates an atmosphere of spiritual mediocrity that paralyzes men's noblest impulses. . . . After a certain level of the problem has been reached, legalistic thinking induces paralysis; it prevents one from seeing the scale and meaning of events.[2]

A covenantal relationship rests on shared commitment to ideas, values, and goals. Such an idea expresses the sacred nature of relationships. In his book, *The Season of Leadership,* David Neidert suggests that every covenant is filled with certain obligations and intentions. Among them are trust, respect, mutual support, accountability, and fidelity. "The all-encompassing element of covenant relationships is fidelity. It is probably the most spiritual and passionate of all covenant characteristics. In a covenantal relationship, fidelity contains the sacred vows that leaders and followers make to each other."[3]

Grace-full leadership rests on the concept that the relationship of leaders and followers is, in its highest expression, covenantal rather than contractual. Such a relationship demands trust and a proper balance between personal motives and how followers are affected by their leaders' decisions.

Trust is fundamental to the success of any leader. Since my brother is a dentist, I was intrigued with a little sign that said, "How to Choose a Dentist You Can Trust." It begins with these words of caution:

Never trust a dentist . . .

> . . . who wears dentures
> . . . who has hairy knuckles
> . . . who chews tobacco and spits into the sink
> . . . who is also a hairdresser
> . . . who says, "This won't hurt"
> . . . who uses the suction hose to empty your pockets

Now there are, of course, many fine dentists, my brother among them. But it is natural to wonder, "Who can I trust?" That question encompasses leadership roles as well.

Trust is foundational in order to win the loyalty and support of those you are trying to lead. Trust not only must be established but also must be maintained. Several key characteristics are necessary to generate and sustain trust.

One is *consistency.* A leader must be a person who can be counted upon day in and day out. This consistency breeds a healthy predictability and confidence. Grace-full leaders are clear and steady. There is no gap between what they say and how they live. Trust is given and nurtured when there is consistency between your words and deeds.

A second characteristic of leaders who engender trust is *dependability.* Leaders are there when it counts. They are ever ready to support and encourage their coworkers. Such leaders are reliable, and reliability builds trust.

Integrity is a third ingredient in the trust equation. Without it, there is no hope for a lasting relationship. Personal and organizational integrity are indispensable.

Trust in a leader allows that person to take charge and set the course and pace without having to take control. That is, these leaders *inspire* others to follow rather than *order* others to follow. They are able to establish and maintain positive relationships with their subordinates and peers.

As the leader demonstrates trust, trust is nurtured. Coworkers have to believe that a leader knows what he or she is doing, and a leader must let coworkers know that he or she trusts them. Peter Drucker has pointed out that the chief object of leadership is the creation of a human community held together by the work bond for a common purpose.[4] That is a grace-full difference.

Trust binds leaders and followers together, and it cannot be mandated or bought—but it can be earned. To be trusted, be trustworthy. Then a new depth of relationship will blossom. In such an environment, honest and candid communication takes root. When there is trust, people will risk speaking their mind. While some might find this threatening, it only serves to strengthen the leader. Feedback from a trusted coworker is a powerful force for good.

When I was a boy, a Russian premier named Nikita Khrushchev often dominated the world stage. During one of his visits to America he was invited to give an address at the Washington Press Club. After his remarks he took some questions. The first question from the floor (submitted in writing through a translator) was, "Today you talked about the hideous rule of your predecessor, Stalin. You were one of his closest aides and colleagues during those years. What were *you* doing all that time?" "Who asked that?" he roared. All 500 faces turned down. "Who asked that?" he insisted. No one responded. "That's what I was doing," he said.[5] It was an insightful moment, illustrating how easy it is for people to remain silent in the presence of powerful leaders.

One of the consequences when there is not an atmosphere of trust is that people do not speak up. They will let leaders make mistakes even when they themselves know better. Trust is at the heart of a covenantal relationship; its benefits to the leader and the led are immense.

Contracts take the place of trust; covenants express it, for trust is at the heart of a covenantal relationship. While most relationships have some elements of both, at some point all relationships become essentially one or the other. Contractual relationships exist because of what people *do* for each other. Covenantal relationships exist because of what people *are* or *mean* to each other.

I see this covenantal idea vividly portrayed near the end of each academic year at the university where I serve. As the semester comes to a close, I participate in one of the many end-of-the-year rituals of the school term. It generally takes place in a lovely banquet room of a fine hotel in Chicago where we gather for the annual Orpheus Choir banquet.

Following the meal, the awards, the slide show, and various expressions of appreciation, a closing prayer is offered. After the prayer, we all stand and form two circles.

This tradition is repeated each year at the Orpheus banquet. Two circles: a small inner circle of graduating seniors, each holding another's hand, facing out, and a larger outer circle of everyone else, the undergrads and a few guests, holding hands, facing inward—so that the folks in both circles can see each other's eyes.

The room grows very quiet. The end is at hand: the end of the evening, the end of a great year together as a choir, and, for the seniors, the end of college life. A pitch pipe softly sounds the note, and together the circles begin to sing: "The Lord bless you and keep you. / The Lord lift His countenance upon you, / And give you peace, / and give you peace. / The Lord make His face to shine upon you / And be gracious unto you" (cf. Num. 6:24-26, KJV).

As the room fills with beautiful music, eyes fill with tears, voices quiver, heads bow. It is a moment of blessing and more. For me, this moment is a pageant that beautifully displays the mission, values, and priorities of the university. It is all here: our tradition of great music and service to the church, the academic preparation that brought this moment to pass, the deep friendships formed across the years, seniors and underclassmen and faculty and administrators joined hand in hand; and then the entire scene is anointed by the melodic offering of an ancient blessing. This living symbol of circles and cycles speaks of the covenant relationship that can exist within a group.

One year not long ago, this annual ritual was slightly modified. After 30 years of service the director of the choir was retiring. So rather than seniors moving to the inner circle to receive the musical benediction, the choir members asked the director and his wife to stand in the middle of the group, and with hands clasped around them, the choir sang their farewell in song.

Standing with the choir members in the outer circle, I looked into the eyes of the director—a graceful, grace-filled leader. This leader was loved and revered, not because he had a contract to teach and lead the choir, but because he had poured out his life in service to those students, and they loved him for it. It was a covenantal moment and a moment filled with grace.

Such is the bond of trust and respect that develops between a grace-full leader and those with whom and for whom he or she works. This bond is sacred, for it reflects how God relates to those who follow Him. He comes to us, not with contract in hand, but with open arms.

He comes not to get, but to give. His approach is not negotiation, but reconciliation. God is not a taskmaster, intent on the daily quota, but one who comes alongside to give strength and help and encouragement.

You can only govern men by serving them. The rule is without exception.
—Victor Cousin

For even the Son of Man did not come to be served, but to serve, and to give his life as a ransom for many.
—Mark 10:45

3

GRACE-*full* LEADERS . . .
view people as ends—not means

Leadership is personal. It is relational, collective, and purposeful. Leadership has to do more with people than techniques and procedures. Getting along with and caring for others is at the heart of grace-full leadership.

One college president joked about university administration, saying it would be great if you didn't have to deal with students or faculty. Surprisingly, some leaders view people as occupational hazards rather than colleagues in reaching an organization's goals and objectives. The industrial revolution and methods of mass production have conditioned leaders and managers to think of individuals almost solely in terms of production.

Henry Ford asked, "Why is it that I always get the whole person, when what I really want is a pair of hands?" That describes the attitude of some leaders. They don't want the person, only what the person can do. People, however, are not machines; they are individuals, created in the image of God. They have value and significance beyond their work. A grace-full leader recognizes and affirms the importance of the whole person.

The personal side of leadership is expressed in at least two fundamental ways. First, every leader is a person with his or her own strengths and weaknesses, desires and needs, history and future. In the final analysis, a leader cannot separate leadership decisions and actions from who he or she is as a person.

Recognizing and accepting one's own personhood should give way to the recognition that those who follow the leader are also persons—with strengths, weaknesses, desires, needs, histories, and futures of their own. From the day a person enters the business world or the life of the church until the day he or she retires from any leadership role, there will be people to deal with. Recognizing that leadership is ultimately personal is fundamental to understanding the heart of a Christian leader.

*Grace-full leaders recognize the dignity
of others and affirm the diversity
of their gifts.*

Leaders in the business environment commonly view people as commodities; another category of raw material; a workforce to be used, managed, and replaced at will. Thus, leaders may take over a business and immediately close plants and displace people.

While occasionally within organizational life things do change and people are displaced, nonetheless, the grace-full leader seeks to foster an environment where people can flourish. Leadership that does not promote the overall welfare of the people involved might appear to be efficient and powerful, but it is not Christian. Grace-full leaders recognize the dignity of others and affirm the diversity of their gifts. Everyone comes with certain gifts—but not the same gifts. A polar bear is as unique as a stingray, but don't ask a polar bear to survive under water or a stingray on polar ice. The challenge is to match the person to the position and need at any given time.

Grace-full leadership is therefore intimate and personal, not just professional. Hierarchy and equality are not mutually exclusive. Hierarchy provides the necessary connections. Equality makes hierarchy responsive and responsible.

For instance, as a grace-full leader, when you walk past the custodian and say, "Hey, Wayne, how ya doin'?" you stop, look at Wayne, and give him the respect of your full attention instead of continuing past him before he has a chance to answer. Sending a memo to employees saying you are important is not effective. Treating them with respect and courtesy is.

When you as a leader set or transform the culture of an organization, you are modeling, every moment, how individuals should respond to one another. Simple observation is one powerful way people learn the values and expectations of an organization. When Albert Schweitzer, the great humanitarian, was asked if he had any advice for parents about bringing up children, he said, "I only have three principles, three basic rules. One, you only teach by example. Two, by example. Three, by example."[1] It's the same pattern an effective leader should use.

Grace-full leaders create an environment where individuals accept one another's weaknesses as well as strengths. In such a workplace, people are encouraged (and perhaps more importantly, allowed) to change, grow, and develop. Grace-full leaders resist labeling others. They refuse to be caught in a web of prejudice or stereotyping that looks for the worst in others rather than the best.

∘━━✦━━∘

Viewing people as ends rather than the means to an end creates a positive and productive environment.

∘━━✦━━∘

Viewing people as ends rather than the means to an end creates a positive and productive environment. Great power is released when one respects and believes in another person. It makes the recipient better as well as the giver. Such an attitude develops grace-filled synergy, which means the whole is more than the sum of the parts. That is the heart of teamwork.

This aspect of grace-full leadership builds on the strengths of others. Delegation, the natural extension of leadership, becomes natural. Others who might appear better in certain areas do not threaten grace-full leaders. Leaders must be willing to learn from others.

The grace-full leader works diligently to ensure that every person feels respected, has a sense of genuine involvement in the mission and life of the organization, and is treated fairly. A leader must be fair, but being fair is difficult. Someone has said, "Leaders don't inflict pain, they bear it." I understand that some of both happens along the way, and therefore we must have grace to transform our relationships into a living canvas that displays the presence of God at work in human life.

On those occasions when a leader must deal firmly with a difficult situation, the grace-full leader is able (and willing) to separate people from the problem. Respect for others, even in the midst of disagreements, is one mark of a Christlike spirit.

Lefty Gomez was a pitcher for the New York Yankees. At the close of a baseball season when the Yankees had won yet another World Series and Lefty had pitched a particularly good game, one reporter asked him how he did it, and this is what he said: "I owe my success to a fast outfield!" This answer was Lefty's way of saying that no matter how good any single player may be, success is not possible without the contributions made by the whole team.

Viewing people as ends, not just means, transforms leadership and organizations. When this change takes place in the heart of a leader, it changes how others respond to his or her leadership. In such an environment, trust takes root, people begin to respond more favorably to one another, joy comes to the surface, and productivity increases.

Max DePree set a high standard in this area when he said, "The first responsibility of a leader is to define reality. The last is to say 'thank you.' In between he's a servant and a debtor."[2]

The attitude of the grace-full leader is positive, optimistic, hopeful, and enthusiastic. There is a spiritual energy present that radiates to those both inside and outside an organization. This positive energy is contagious. It dispels negativism and destructive thinking.

A proper view of others keeps one's view of power in line as well. Leadership is power, but it is a particular kind of power. Grace-full leadership resists the temptation to rely on coercive power. Coercive power rests on fear. The leader may fear that others won't follow or accept him or her without coercion. And followers fear the retribution of the leader who seeks to coerce compliance. The result is an abuse of power that imposes a psychological and emotional burden on followers and leaders alike.

Others exert a utilitarian power. Leaders are followed because in doing so, followers have access to certain benefits and opportunities. Stephen Covey observes: "The compliance that is based on utility power tends to look more like influence than control."[3] There is a sense in which this type of power is similar to coercion, but it is a positive rather than a negative force. In the coercive model a follower seeks to avoid some negative response, while in the utilitarian model, he or she seeks to gain a positive benefit.

A third alternative might be called the natural power of leadership. It is natural in that it does not seek followers based only on threat or reward. Natural power rests upon the motivation of a worthy goal and a common good. The motivation to follow rests (at least in part) beyond the follower himself or herself. The power is created when the values of the followers and the values of the leader overlap.

The natural power base can only be developed in a setting where people are viewed as important and valuable in and of themselves—apart from what they might contribute to the bottom line. This is the product of grace and patience. It is not easy, but the rewards are great for both the leader and the followers. The leader is honored and respected and thus more effective over time. The follower is valued, affirmed, and thus more motivated to work for the good of the organization and in support of the leader.

Grace-full leaders are quick to pass along praise and recognize the contributions made by other people.

A good leader is someone who does not monopolize credit. Grace-full leaders are quick to pass along praise and recognize the contributions made by other people. They seek to be inclusive by sharing ideas, associations, and benefits as widely as possible. The grace-full leader is generous. He or she has no need to manipulate others or practice a kind of leadership by intimidation.

Communication with others must be timely, direct, and clear. In addition, leaders must also foster an environment of empowerment. Don't let that word throw you! Some are threatened by the thought of empowering others. But empowerment should strengthen and extend your leadership rather than threaten it. This was the pattern of Jesus with His disciples. He sought to take followers and make leaders out of them. He promised, "Anyone who has faith in me will do what I have been doing. He will do even greater things than these" (John 14:12).

Warren Bennis suggests that empowering people is not only something a leader might do but also an "obligation of leaders to coach people to bring out their potential, to really be people growers."[4]

Leaders not only accept and have confidence in themselves but also accept and think well of others. Sincerity and positive regard for others simply cannot be faked, and one needs both to deal with people effectively. To be a grace-full leader, one must take the words of Jesus' great commandment to heart: "Love the Lord your God with all your heart and with all your soul and with all your mind" and "Love your neighbor as yourself" (Matt. 22:37, 39). The guiding principle of this commandment is a simple value and respect for one another.

Dr. Bob Brower, the president of Point Loma Nazarene University in San Diego, wrote an article for that school's alumni publication in which he tells this story:

Recently, I got trapped in one of those automated phone systems as I was trying to reach a person in an organization whose business is people-focused. After more than three minutes of punching options and trying to reach the individual I was calling, I finally got an option that said, "For personal attention, dial zero." Greatly relieved to finally have the hope of reaching a real live person, I pressed "0" and waited. After some clicking and electronic rerouting, the automated voice came back on and said, "We're sorry, personal attention is not available." Yes, I laughed, hung up, and thought about the all-too-frequent experience of an age marked by the impersonal.[5]

For a genuine, grace-full leader, no one should be put on hold, no one ignored, and no one left unloved. Leadership should serve as a prism through which the true and transforming light of God is refracted and thus falls with color and grace in every direction. Only through God's grace can we become leaders who treat people as ends, not means.

When people become involved in the problem, they become significantly and sincerely committed to coming up with solutions to the problem.
—Stephen R. Covey

Forget the former things; do not dwell on the past. See, I am doing a new thing!
—Isa. 43:18-19

4

GRACE-*full* LEADERS . . .
recognize the changeable from the changeless

Things change. A challenge in leadership is to accept and manage change without altering what is most vital to the health of an organization. In the midst of change, grace-full leaders hold on to and preserve the heart and essence of an organization's identity.

Things change. The little church building where I went with my family as a child has been replaced with a beautiful new structure at the edge of town. The building was already old when I was young; it was small and hot and worn and tired. It had several previous owners before our congregation occupied it—but it served its purpose well and was eventually replaced.

Programs, materials, resources, and technology have all changed as well. I was eight or nine when the first singing group with a P.A. system visited our church. I remember the musicians carrying in speakers, microphones, stands, and what seemed like endless cords of wiring. It created a considerable stir, and I thought this was quite a happening. The adults, however, weren't too sure. It seemed a little "worldly" to them. During Sunday dinner that day, my father said, "Well, they were pretty good, but it did seem a little too 'show-businessy.'" However, over time we learned that technology could be used for the glory of God. Today the church is blanketing the world with radio, television, film, and computer technology.

Even people change—CEOs, supervisors, pastors, superintendents, teachers, and college presidents come and go. And yet organizations can and often do flourish even in the face of such personnel changes, for although change brings with it certain uncertainties, it also brings a host of new possibilities. The leadership issue rests, not in the effort to shelter the organization from change, but rather in the ability to manage, lead, and capitalize on the certainty of change.

If the followers are to respond positively,
the leader must first accept the pace and
necessity of change.

Resistance as well as opportunity usually accompany change. How well you manage that dynamic tension will determine the effectiveness of your leadership. Grace-full leaders recognize that change is both necessary and inevitable and that it brings with it obstacles that must be recognized and managed.

Change can be a genuine opportunity for renewal, but the problem is that "change has no constituency." That is to say, most people do not like change. Change often means letting go of things that are familiar and moving into unknown territory. Even when a person does not like things as they are, he or she may still find it hard to venture into the unknown. In order to successfully determine what should change and what should not, and then to effectively manage those things, you must first be comfortable with the realities of change in your own life. If the followers are to respond positively, the leader must first accept the pace and necessity of change.

Change must not be viewed as the enemy, for only by changing can an organization survive over time and thrive in an environment that is in constant flux. Change is not the enemy; changing the wrong things is. It takes grace to know the difference.

Too often leaders try hard to force change by simply declaring, "This is the way it will be." Or they attempt to micromanage the organization through a period of change. A better option is to create a new vision, based on a clear understanding of reality, and let that vision bring about a natural change.

Effective leadership shapes people's opinions and wins their enthusiasm. Leadership is, at least in part, salesmanship; getting people to say, "C'mon, we can do this." Stephen Covey has noted that "almost every significant breakthrough is the result of a courageous break with traditional ways of thinking."[1]

Change is more natural and positive if the people affected by it are also involved in determining and implementing the change. As human beings we tend to be more interested in our own ideas rather than those of others. If we are not involved, we will likely resist change.

To be an effective change agent, a leader must often create a story or a vision of the future that will draw others in the organization into the new possibilities. John Kotter, from the Harvard Business School, gives a very simple description of this in his book *Leading Change.*

Imagine the following. Three groups of ten individuals are in a park at lunchtime with a rainstorm threatening. In the first group, someone says: "Get up and follow me." When he starts walking and only a few others join in, he yells to those still seated: "Up, I said, and NOW!" In the second group, someone says: "We're going to have to move. Here's the plan. Each of us stands up and marches in the direction of the apple tree. Please stay at least two feet away from other group members and do not run. Do not leave any personal belongings on the ground here and be sure to stop at the base of the tree. When we are all there . . ." In the third group, someone tells the others: "It's going to rain in a few minutes. Why don't we go over there and sit under the apple tree. We'll stay dry, and we can have fresh apples for lunch."[2]

The illustration is a simple one, but the principle is sound. An effective leader recognizes changes in the environment that might precipitate changes within the organization and immediately begins to communicate those shifts and suggest alternatives. When this is carried out effectively, change becomes the natural response.

Managing change is one demand of leadership; recognizing that things should not change is another.

Managing change is one demand of leadership; recognizing that things should *not* change is another. Through the rhythms of leadership, the grace-full leader recognizes the eternal nature of certain principles and priorities that must be nurtured even through times of change.

Built to Last is a book by James C. Collins and Jerry Porras that identifies and describes the habits of visionary companies able to adapt effectively to change. It flows from extensive research. One of the most significant observations in the book is the vital role of an organization's ability to change while still preserving its essential identity. At one point the authors write:

> The fundamental distinguishing characteristic of the most enduring and successful corporations is that they preserve a cherished core ideology while simultaneously stimulating progress and change in everything that is not part of their core ideology. . . . In truly great companies, change is constant, but not the only constant. They understand the difference between what should never change and what should be open for change, between what is truly sacred and what is not. And by being clear about what should never change, they are better able to stimulate change and progress in everything else.[3]

Several years ago, I had the privilege to be a postdoctoral resident fellow at Harvard. It was a rich and rewarding experience. Nearly every day during my time there I walked from our apartment on Mount Auburn Street to the Harvard Divinity School on the other side of campus.

My daily trek took me through the Johnson Gate and into Harvard Yard, past Massachusetts Hall built in the mid-1700s, and out through the Emerson Gate. In the distance the bronze statue of John Harvard watched my daily pilgrimage.

I walked on past Sanders Auditorium and Sparks House. I cut down a side street past the Peabody Museum of Cultural Anthropology, through a little passageway between two buildings, and on to Andover Hall, the main building of the Divinity School complex.

I was there to study at Harvard, but I also wanted to study Harvard itself. So I took time to read Henry Rosovsky's book titled *The University: An Owner's Manual* and Richard Norton Smith's *Harvard Century: The Making of a University*. I wanted to understand what made the place tick and, particularly, why the Harvard of today is so different from its beginnings.

Within 18 years of the Pilgrims setting foot on Plymouth Rock the first, and perhaps most famous, school in America was founded. The early story is etched today in the record of Harvard. The charter of the school says: "After God carried us safely to New England, and we had built our houses, provided for our livelihood, reared convenient places for God's worship, and settled the civil government; one of the next things we longed for and looked after was to advance learning, and perpetuate it to posterity; dreading to leave an illiterate ministry to the churches, when our present ministers shall lie in the dust."[4]

With great optimism this colony of 12,000 people, 2,500 miles and an ocean away from the nearest university, established a college to advance learning. On November 20, 1637, a board of governors was established. The site for the new school was the little village of Newtowne, which was immediately renamed Cambridge because most of the magistrates were graduates of Cambridge University in England.

The early documents declare, "Spiritual learning is our chief desire, for it shall sanctify the other."

The overseers purchased a large holding pen, actually a cattle yard, where the livestock were kept at night. That became Harvard Yard.

The college opened under the leadership of Nathan Eton in the summer of 1638. In December of that year, John Harvard, a resident of nearby Charlestown, died at just 31. He left the college half of his estate and his entire library. In recognition of this generosity the new college at Cambridge was named Harvard College.

One early leader of Harvard, a man named Increase Mather, challenged the students to "find a friend in truth." That quest for *veritas* became the slogan for Harvard and is the motto yet today.

In the early days they knew where to find truth. Harvard's first presidents and faculty members insisted that there could be no true knowledge or wisdom without Jesus Christ. Harvard's "Rules and Precepts" adopted in 1646 included the following statement: "Every one shall consider the main end of his life and studies to know God and Jesus Christ which is eternal life."

If the mission of an institution is clearly and pervasively renewed, reembraced, revived, then there results a kind of new beginning.

Across the years not only Harvard's campus changed but also its inner workings. Its worthy goal gave way, through a series of small and probably not so small decisions. Mission was lost in the maze of institutional compromise. As the torch was passed, the light flickered rather than flamed.

Scholars note that there is a historic drift in all institutions, moving them from being mission-driven to maintenance-driven. Those who study such things suggest that this institutional arthritis cannot be prevented—it is a natural part of the aging process. It can, at best, only be retarded.

With one exception, I think they are right. That is the possibility of mission renewal. If the mission of an institution is clearly and pervasively renewed, reembraced, revived, then there results a kind of new beginning, and the cycle starts over.

The grace-full leader must have the capacity to adapt to change and even facilitate change, without eroding the essence of the organization or entity he or she leads.

The story of change is part of every person's story. The question is not "Will we change?" but "In what ways will we change?"

What are the factors that shape and mold us? Some of those forces are outside our control, but there are also forces at work within us:

the desires
        and drives
              and dreams
                    and daily decisions
from which our character flows. Grace-full leaders learn to distinguish the changeable from the changeless.

My motivation for daily work must be a desire to serve God as a steward
of the earth and a steward of my own talents and aptitudes.
—Robert Slocum

Whatever you do, work at it with all your heart,
as working for the Lord, not for men.
—Col. 3:23

5

GRACE-*full* LEADERS . . .
seek significance, not just success

In the business world, success of an organization is measured by profit and net worth. That's the bottom line. That is success, and it is a valid measurement. However, it's not the only measure of success. Grace-full leadership seeks significance as well as bottom-line success.

While stumping for election to the U.S. House of Representatives, in a speech given near Bloomington, Illinois, Abraham Lincoln told of a little locomotive that was used on a small section of track near Springfield. The engine had one dominant point of pride: it supported a huge whistle that could be heard, it was said, all up and down the Sangamon River Valley.

The locomotive, however, had one dominant problem. The whistle was so large and the boiler so small that the engineer often had to make a decision: whether to sound the whistle or pull the load, for he could not do both at once. On occasion leaders may feel that they, too, must decide between the two competing values: success or significance. But it doesn't have to be an either/or situation. In fact, in the best scenario, success and significance are joined as complimentary sides of the same coin.

Grace-full leaders keep their focus on what is primary. That focus is far more significant than the normal measurements of success. Christian leaders understand the concepts and philosophy of management by objectives, yet see beyond the focus on outcomes to a style and philosophy of leadership that is actually management by values as well as objectives. Simply reaching your goals and business objectives is not enough. True significance comes when you reach those objectives with your values still intact.

What you do certainly has value beyond the immediate. Success means little if it is not lasting. Grace-full leadership seeks enduring results. It is the difference, for example, between earning a degree and getting an education. While receiving a degree is a sign and measure of academic success, the significance of that accomplishment is the education received.

Significance comes from working with others who are not only associates but also friends. Like most things, the joy of success comes from the journey toward it even more than the accomplishment of it. A few years ago our football team at the university where I serve played for the national championship. It was a great moment. That game was a symbol of success for both the coaches and the players.

After the season ended, I attended the annual football banquet. As the awards were given, including the recognition of one or two all-Americans on our team, the overriding theme of the celebration was not so much the accomplishment as the teamwork and friendships and memories of it all. The true significance of that football season was what those players had experienced, not what they had accomplished. They will draw fresh water from that well of experience for years to come.

⊶

I know people living in wonderful houses who are still struggling to establish a home.

⊶

The difference between success and significance is like the difference between a house and a home. To live in a grand house is often considered a sign of success. However, I know people living in wonderful houses who are still struggling to establish a home. While in graduate school during the early years of our marriage my wife, Jill, and I moved several times. The places we lived were always modest, but each soon became home to us as we filled the place, day after day, with the living of our lives. Over time, each little house or apartment became a significant place to us because of the experiences we shared while living there. Which is better, a great house or a great home? It is possible to have both; but if you have to choose, most would choose the home, for in the long run that is the more significant possession.

Significance comes from performing a work worth doing and executing it well. *How the job is done* is as significant in some cases as *that the job is done.* I mentioned the variety of apartments and houses Jill and I lived in when we were young adults. One of our goals with each move was to add a bit of color with a few fresh decorating touches. Often it was the addition of wallpaper. Hanging wallpaper is one activity that provides a significant test of a marriage relationship. Jill says that the reason wall papering was so stressful was that one of us simply wanted it on the wall while the other wanted it straight! To me, simply getting the wallpaper on the wall (and having it stay there) was a success. To her, having it straight was significant.

As I look back, I can see that taking the time to do it right, to get it straight and have it match perfectly, added to the value of what we did. Not only did the final product look better, but also it made us feel better about our work and ourselves.

Quality of work is a primary concern for grace-full leaders. Poor work becomes a disservice to God and the world around us, and it diminishes the significance of the labor. How a job is done is significant.

Significance also flows from making the world a better place. Work must have some importance beyond itself. Others must benefit from our labor if we are to know the joy of significance. Closely related to this idea is the responsibility to be involved in the mission of social reform.

"Often the world of work is characterized by less-than-Christian values, and workers individually or as groups need to prophetically challenge such injustices as degrading working conditions, faulty products, poor-quality work, mismanagement of the firm, or waste of other people's money."[1] The gospel and the presence of a Christian in the social context can and should make a powerful difference in how others are treated.

Celebrations connect individuals to the higher values present in one's working environment.

Significance must be regularly affirmed and even celebrated within the life of an organization. Celebrations connect individuals to the higher values present in one's working environment. I recently participated in a celebration, a special luncheon, for an employee who had completed 20 years of service in a given department. The lunch was not sponsored by the organization, but it was planned and conducted by this individual's coworkers.

The celebration of 20 years of service was not about productivity or success in terms of meeting quotas and so on. It was a celebration of the significance of a person's 20-year devotion to a worthy cause. It was an observance focused on the deep relationships formed across those years and the influence of this one individual in the lives of colleagues and customers. It was a moment that said, "You and your work are significant." Such moments weave our work and hearts together.

The people of the workplace are part of the significance. Working to the glory of God is not just an issue of being diligent on the job but also includes being loving and redemptive in relationship with those with whom and for whom we work.

Work in and of itself can be significant and bestow value. "That man should work is as much a part of the regular order of things as that the sun should rise or that lions should hunt: 'man goeth forth to his work and to his labor until evening'" (cf. Ps. 104:19-23, KJV).[2]

*Men and women are called to be
new creations in Christ.*

The Old Testament teaches that work is to be regarded as a necessary, worthy, and, indeed, a God-appointed function of human life. "The basic assumption of the biblical viewpoint is that work is a divine ordinance for the life of man."[3] The fourth commandment is a command to rest from labor, based upon the biblical idea that man and woman are workers by nature.

Biblical writers recognized the dignity of work and the expectation that people should work. Work is not to be understood as a result of the Fall or as a punishment from God. Before the Fall, humankind was created to "fill the earth and subdue it. Rule over the fish of the sea and the birds of the air and over every living creature that moves on the ground" (Gen. 1:28). Certainly work, like all of life, has been affected by the fall of humans, but it remains throughout the Scripture as part of God's plan and purpose for humankind. Work itself brings added significance to life.

In the New Testament it becomes clear that although we must work, our primary calling (vocation) is to repentance, faith, fellowship, and service. Men and women are called to be new creations in Christ. This call to *be* precedes the calling to *do*. The Bible doesn't indicate that God calls us to an earthly profession or trade. Paul, for example, is called by God to be an apostle; he is not "called" to be a tentmaker.[4]

This does not mean, however, that secular employment is of no concern to Christians. It simply underscores that being a worker in a vocational sense is secondary to the higher calling of God in Christ. This means that occupations are not ends in themselves, but part of our means to fulfill and express our primary calling as the people of God. So the significance of work is in great measure determined by how God is glorified and how the kingdom of God is advanced through labor.

As a means of witnessing and expressing one's faith, the New Testament calls upon believers to be honest and faithful in their work. "Whatever you do, work at it with all your heart, as working for the Lord, not for men" (Col. 3:23). This calls the people of God to affirm that Jesus is the Lord of their vocational lives and to offer the quality of their work to the Lord as an expression of their devotion and stewardship.

Work has significance beyond itself and can be recognized as a divine mandate and ministry

Elton Trueblood noted that we make a serious mistake if we think that work is not Christian unless it is work for the churches. "Actually the witness made in regular employment may be far more significant and productive than any service rendered in free time."[5] Work is not to be considered a curse but a calling. It is a way to construct a better world in union with Christ.

Work has significance beyond itself and can be recognized as a divine mandate and ministry. "Work is a search for enduring meaning as well as for daily bread, for recognition as well as for pay, for service to others as well as for one's self-worth and pride."[6]

Work is part of what it means to be human and it is through the sanctifying of their work that people find work's true dignity and meaning. The value of work lies beyond the particular nature of the work being done. Its value lies in sharing in God's purposes as expressed through work. Human labor is an "occasion for people to cooperate with God and share in God's creative work."[7]

The temptation for many believers is to center their lives around the activities and programs of the local church rather than seeing their mission to be in the world of work for the glory of God. Christians must see that it is in the daily labors of their working life that they, "the people of God," are in the center of the arena where the Church needs to be.

Robert Slocum gives five guidelines for helping integrate faith and vocational work.[8] The first guideline refers to the recognition that work is a divine mandate. God planned for work to be an important part of our lives. "Because work originated with God, it follows that we are to look at work as something to which God calls us and as something he can use to give divine order to our lives."[9]

A second principle concerns a person's motivation for work. A Christian's highest motivation for work should not be the material benefits but the witness and ministry provided through the avenue of work. "My motivation for daily work must be a desire to serve God as a steward of the earth and a steward of my own talents and aptitudes."[10]

Next, the issue of career goals and future relationship to vocation is addressed by the following guideline: "I must accept the fact that my unfolding future in my daily work is in God's hands."[11] This probes the issue of whether or not you are willing to set aside personal goals or corporate goals to understand God's plans and purposes.

The fourth guideline speaks to the need for a strong sense of stewardship to pervade your understanding of the role of work in God's plans for men and women. "Even if the future is in God's hands, I have in my own hands the stewardship responsibility for developing my own talents, aptitudes, and abilities.

This fourth guideline means that God can guide and direct my work life as I work at being a good steward of my personal resources."[12]

Here individuals are called upon to make sure they are using their God-given talents and opportunities to the best of their abilities. The individual question is, "How can I develop and invest my aptitudes and skills as an act of responsible obedience to Jesus Christ?"

∘━✦━∘

The hours spent at work can become
"Kingdom hours" that provide a
powerful witness to the world
of the grace and glory of God.

∘━✦━∘

The final guideline has to do with expectations of success and rewards. Simply stated, the guideline is this: "It is up to God whether and how I am blessed."[13] Vocational success cannot be measured on the standards of this world alone. Our work and the results of our work must continually be yielded to God.

"Life proves itself Christian in the happenings of one's working life."[14] A strong part of a Christian's commitment to serve God is seen in his or her integration of faith and vocational work. The Christian life and witness are severely hampered without this integration. "God cannot be loved in opposition to our daily working life, nor apart from it, but only served in it. In their work laity use their talents, show their virtues, and prove their fidelity."[15]

So faith makes a difference in how one views work and how one works. Bringing the gospel to all of life can flood a person's working hours with new meaning and new potential. The hours spent at work can become "Kingdom hours" that provide a powerful witness to the world of the grace and glory of God. It is vital to the church, the individual, and the world at large that a true integration of faith and work take place in the life of every believer. As this happens, success gives way to significance.

Response-ability is the ability to choose our response to any circumstance or condition. When we are response-able, our commitment becomes more powerful than our moods or circumstances, and we keep the promises and resolutions we make.
—Stephen R. Covey

The people rejoiced at the willing response of their leaders, for they had given freely and wholeheartedly to the Lord.
—1 Chron. 29:9

6
GRACE-*full* LEADERS . . .
are responsive as well as responsible

To be responsible is to take care of business. If a leader is not responsible, neither he nor she nor the organization will survive, much less flourish. Taking responsibility is essential. It is "the buck stops here" ingredient of leadership. But being responsible is not enough. Leaders must also be responsive. To be responsive is to be able to step outside of one's leadership role and assess the total environment. The responsive leader learns to adjust plans, procedures, and policies to accommodate changes and organizational concerns.

Not many people had heard of the town Methuen, Massachusetts, until the fire. It was a company town. The community looked to Malden Mills, which employed nearly 2,400 people, for most of its prosperity and security. Malden Mills had known good and bad days. But now, through the strong leadership of its owner, Aaron Feuerstein, and the innovation of its research team, the factory was doing extremely well. It had successfully made the transition from a business dependent on traditional ways and products to the development of a very light, yet warm and wildly popular, product known as "polar fleece," made from recycled plastic bottles.

That December, like folks all across America, the residents of this little village were getting ready for Christmas. The downtown was lit with colored lights. Christmas trees, angels, and Santas adorned the shops and restaurants. Everything seemed very peaceful: then, without warning, the boiler at the plant exploded, destroying three of the factory's buildings and turning the hopes and dreams of hundreds of people to ashes.

Aaron Feuerstein quickly began to assess the damage. The destruction was extensive. Feuerstein's advisers suggested that he take the insurance money and use this opportunity to move much of his manufacturing business to a third-world setting. It could be done for a fraction of what he had been paying locally. But that was not his reaction.

Aaron Feuerstein called for his employees to meet at the local school gymnasium. The air was heavy with the weight of tragedy and the fog of an uncertain future as Feuerstein entered the building. He shook the snow from his boots and walked to the platform. He lifted his head and with a calm voice announced that the factory would be rebuilt and that everyone would be paid for the next month (a benefit he continued month by month for the next several months). His employees were awestruck. They laughed and cried, prayed and celebrated.

Here was a leader who was both responsible and responsive. His bold action created hope and possibility. In an interview Aaron Feuerstein said,

When people saw the devastation, they were positive that this seventy-year-old owner would collect the insurance and just say good-bye, but we do not operate that way. We are going to operate with whatever strength we can until we have again established Malden Mills as the leader in the industry. My father told me of the ancient Rabbi Hillel, who advised that in a situation that is devoid of morality, try to be a man and do something worthwhile. I haven't really done anything. I don't deserve credit. Corporate America has made it so that when you do behave the way I did, it's abnormal.[1]

A grace-full leader is not only responsible but also responsive to the human equation, to all employees and their families, and to the community at large.

Being responsive means that a leader is able to adjust to any unforeseen obstacle or opportunity with the flexibility to respond and not just react. Such a characteristic is vital in the 21st-century world of change and unpredictability.

Equilibrium between being responsible and responsive is necessary. Leaders must be able to guide organizations that seek to maintain and preserve their identities, corporate cultures, and traditions while responding to the forces of change. "Successful organizations must find ways to balance the need for adaptation with the need for stability."[2]

Leaders must see feedback, evaluation and assessment, and even criticism as avenues toward success, not failure.

Responsive leaders do not run from feedback, they run toward it. By knowing what is happening and what is not happening in an organization, a leader can determine when and how to respond. Lack of timely feedback kills the frog in the classic illustration of a frog placed in a beaker of cool water that is ever so slowly being heated. The change is so gradual and the frog's internal systems so unresponsive that it sits in the water until it dies from the heat. Leaders must see feedback, evaluation and assessment, and even criticism as avenues toward success, not failure.

Years ago a fellow I know bought an imported car. He lived in a rural area where the specialized service for such a car was simply not available. Once a year he drove 100 miles to the city where he bought the car in order for a trained mechanic to service and check his vehicle and make any necessary adjustments. On occasion, in between those yearly trips, his car would develop some internal problem, and it would trigger a light on the dashboard. My friend's method of testing whether or not the problem was serious was to simply keep driving the car. He reasoned that if it still runs, the problem couldn't be too serious. More than once he put a piece of tape over the warning light and just kept driving, putting his car and himself at risk.

Every year businesses fail, organizations flounder, institutions decline. Is it possible that there are no lights flashing on the dashboard of those companies? More likely, the light is flashing, but no one thinks it's very serious or part of his or her responsibility. Only organizations with responsive leaders can survive over the long haul.

During my first year as a college president, I visited Dean L. Hubbard, the president of Northwest Missouri State University. He was a seasoned president, an original thinker, and an innovative leader. I went initially to see the technological innovations underway at Northwest at that time. Dean Hubbard was well ahead of the curve on the development of campus computer networks. He and his staff at the university were modeling ways to respond to the emerging technology.

During my visit, I caught a vision of what I thought should be done technologically at the school where I serve, but I received more than that. I secured a commitment from President Hubbard to make a visit to our campus. In the next few months he made several visits and agreed to conduct an academic audit for us.

○━━◆━━○

Being responsive allows an organization to discontinue practices no longer effective.

○━━◆━━○

His audit was instructive in two significant ways. First, and most obviously, he was able to determine, through a careful analysis of our records, that certain departments were very productive and efficient, and others were, in fact, lagging seriously behind institutional expectations. Hubbard's study showed that the credit hours of one or two departments, which consumed significant institutional resources, had been steadily declining over the past few years. You might think that it would have been obvious, but because many faculty members teach in various related departments, the trends weren't apparent on the surface. As a result of the study, the *light on the dashboard* began flashing, saying this area needs servicing: it may need repair.

Being responsive allows an organization to discontinue practices no longer effective. Most good ideas and effective methods run their course in time and need to be replaced with other good ideas and effective methods. The "we've always done it that way" attitude is often hard to overcome because the weight of tradition and organizational history supports the tried-and-true ways of the past. The responsive leader has the ability to recognize when new outcomes are needed and when old methods may not be sufficient.

Responsive leaders understand that leadership is dynamic and fluid, not stagnant. It is important that a leader develops the capacity to see things in a wide perspective and receives impressions and gains experiences directly, not vicariously. These impressions will point beyond the experiences and data themselves to issues of continuity and purpose.

Robert McNamara, as secretary of defense in the Johnson administration, directed most of the details of the Vietnam War. He was a good man who was assigned a great responsibility. However, over time he emerged as a leader preoccupied with the minutiae of war planning. His focus was on trying to ensure efficiency and effectiveness half a world away. That is what a good leader does—but that's not all a good leader should do. A leader ought to also recognize the moral dilemmas that surround and accompany the actions.

Grace-full leaders must have one foot firmly placed on the rock of responsibility and a second planted in the stable soil of responsiveness. Leadership takes a good measure of both and the wisdom of knowing when and how to distinguish between them. "People in positions of authority must be alert, curious, impatient, brave, steadfast, truthful, and in focus; they must not only know what they see but say what they see. Gandhi said, 'We must be the change we wish to see in the world.' Thus, if people in authority believe that competence and conscience must be restored, then they must demonstrate both."[3]

Leaders must do more than manage, more than tinker with the machinery or rearrange the administrative furniture on the deck of the ship. The responsive leader has an entrepreneurial spirit. In addition to being unafraid to ask the hard questions, he or she is unafraid of hearing the answers and responding to them with fresh vision and creative ideas.

Harold Green, former president of ITT, says that over the years American management has lost its zest for adventure, for taking a risk, for doing something that no one has done before. Behind this change is the mistaken belief that professional business managers are supposed to be sure of themselves and never make a mistake. Leaders can overcome this tendency by creating an environment where failure is not final, where one admits his or her mistakes, learns from them, and moves on with confidence. Fear of failure will paralyze a leader.

Finally, for responsive leadership to flourish, grace-full leaders must be listening leaders. The first step in making an appropriate response is to listen. A leader must be willing—even anxious—to hear, consider, and accept ideas from others.

Too many people view listening as a passive activity. It is not. Listening is an intensely active and personal pursuit. Grace-full leaders listen with their ears, eyes, and hearts. They hear the words, but they listen for more than what is said. They seek to understand why it was said, what it meant, and how they should respond.

To listen well, you must set aside preconceived notions, prejudices, and your personal agenda. You must learn to listen and listen to learn. In many ways listening is the primary response of the responsive leader.

The fullness or emptiness of life will be measured by the extent to which a person feels that he/she has an impact on the lives of others.
—Kingman Brewster

And surely I am with you always, to the very end of the age.
—Matt. 28:20

7

GRACE-*full* LEADERS . . .
are high-touch

My hometown in Ohio, like a lot of small towns in the U.S., is divided into two sections by a railroad track. Often, when I was growing up, all of the east-west traffic in town (both cars) would come to a standstill as a train passed through. We learned to live with that arrangement and never really thought much about it, for there weren't that many trains nor that many cars.

On one sunny Memorial Day, however, our annual community parade was winding its way through town. The staging area for those in the parade was at the north end of Second Street at the city park. When all were assembled, the various groups would march south a few blocks and then turn west onto Main Street, head through town and arrive at Maple Hill Cemetery for a brief ceremony.

The parade was pretty modest by big-city standards. It consisted of the local Boy Scouts and Girl Scouts, the American Legion and the VFW, the mayor in a convertible, an antique car or two, a few tissue-decorated floats, the high school band, and a host of pets tagging along.

Somehow, though, on this particular day, the drum major, who was leading the band as they marched, got out a little farther than normal in front of the musicians. The band wasn't playing; there was just the drum cadence. The drum major strutted on ahead, crossing the railroad tracks some distance ahead of the band. Just after he cleared the tracks, the black-and-white crossing gates slowly began to lower, and the band came to an abrupt halt. However, the drum major had noticed none of this—he was in a world of his own. There he was, marching down the street, blowing his whistle and waving his great baton, but no one at all was following him.

Leadership can be like that if one fails to stay in touch. As the most visible person in the parade, the leader sets the cadence and points the way. But he or she must, at the same time, be careful not to let too much distance get between him or her and those who are following. For the truth is, the folks gathered along the parade route are not there to see the drum major; they have come to hear the music, and the music is being made by the members of the band.

Grace-full leadership is "high-touch" in at least four dimensions: staying in touch with (1) yourself, (2) the internal and external environment in which you must function, (3) those whom you lead, and (4) God.

Staying in Touch with Yourself

Leadership is a deeply personal business. You must be able to bring out the best in yourself before you can bring out the best in others, so it's important to be in touch with your strengths and weaknesses, needs and desires.

It might seem as if it's supposed to be "natural" to stay in touch with yourself, but sometimes what a leader wants from life is not the same as what he or she is actually experiencing. Indications of this include burnout, breakdown, depression, and midlife crises.

Staying in touch with yourself involves listening to your own self-talk, evaluating your moods and unguarded reactions, and paying attention to physical symptoms. Take some time for reflection. Every leader should do a time audit occasionally. Log the use of your time over an extended period. Then review the record and ask: "Am I pleased with how I use my time? Am I giving myself to the most important things in my life?"

A leader should have a clear set of written goals and priorities and review them regularly. Build into your schedule times for self-audits, and carefully review your work and life.

Leaders also need a person or two who will provide direct feedback. I have asked a faculty and a staff member on our campus to feel empowered to talk directly to me if they observe behaviors or responses from me that do not seem consistent with my stated professional and personal goals and objectives.

Staying in Touch with Your Environment

The person who is successful in leadership, particularly over time, stays in touch with internal changes within the organization: market trends, new technologies, improved methods and products. Such leaders also stay in touch with ideas and advice of others. "It is only by staying in touch with the world around them that leaders can ever expect to change the business-as-usual environment."[1]

*In order to stay in touch, you must
establish relationships, connect with key
sources of information, and simply get
out and walk around.*

In order to stay in touch, you must establish relationships, connect with key sources of information, and simply get out and walk around. Only through human contact can change, innovation, and responsiveness happen.

Staying in touch may include continuing education, either formally (taking classes, attending seminars) or informally (reading and careful observation). Leaders are learners, and it's a lifelong pursuit. "In a time of drastic change, it is the learners who inherit the future. The learned find themselves equipped to live in a world that no longer exists."[2] This quotation from Eric Hoffer underscores three important concepts. One is the basic need for education. Second is the recognition of the rapid pace of change. Third is the necessity of lifelong learning. Learning is a key part of staying in touch with the changing world around us.

Staying in Touch with Others

Staying in touch with others provides a network to accomplish your goals and nurture your spirit. Both functions are vital. You cannot lead effectively at arm's length; it takes face-to-face interaction and support. John Maxwell speaks of The Law of Connection, saying that leaders touch a heart before they ask for a hand.[3] The deeper the relationship between a leader and those who follow, the more effective your leadership becomes.

The people in our lives are vital to our existence, growth, and development. By focusing on tasks and projects, quotas and objects, technology and productivity, a leader can unknowingly become isolated from the people in daily life. It's not that you don't have contact and talk or interact with others, but it is that those interactions are confined to the surface.

Grace-full leaders know how to distinguish between groups and individuals who are in groups. It's a matter of seeing past organizational structure to the people who comprise the organization. The university where I work doesn't exist without the people who comprise the faculty, staff, students, and constituents. To be an effective leader, I must stay in touch with these people. It seems so simple, yet it is one of the greatest challenges of leadership—to keep from getting out of touch.

This can happen at home as well as at work. If your emotional and physical energy is spent on so many tasks and projects at work, it can affect relationships at home. Staying connected takes energy, time, and effort. Left unattended and/or taken for granted, relationships deteriorate. But investing in the relationships of family and friends brings magnificent returns in refreshment and encouragement, and in the end you are more productive by taking time away from work to stay in touch with others. The grace-full leader resists losing touch by nurturing the people side of leadership and life.

Staying in Touch with God

Not long ago, I was returning to campus one Saturday afternoon. I switched on the car radio to try to catch our campus broadcast of a home football game. At first there was nothing but static, so I checked the dial. It was set to the right frequency, but still no voice, no message, no words—just static.

Still driving in the direction of the university, I began to hear the voice of our sports broadcaster. I couldn't hear him very well at first, just a word or two. In fact, I thought for quite a while that our team was leading, when really we were behind. Hearing the wrong message is almost worse than not hearing anything at all. But as I neared home, the message became clearer. Other signals, the static, and foreign voices all gave way to the clear signal from WONU.

The principle is that you must be tuned to the right signal and move closer each moment to the one who is broadcasting. Leaders need to do the same in their relationship with God. They must tune in and keep moving closer to God. In the busy pace of life you might hear only part of what God wants to say—just a word here and there through the static of life.

Jesus talked specifically with His followers about staying in touch. He said,

> Remain in me, and I will remain in you. No branch can bear fruit by itself; it must remain in the vine. Neither can you bear fruit unless you remain in me.
>
> I am the vine; you are the branches. If a man remains in me and I in him, he will bear much fruit; apart from me you can do nothing. If anyone does not remain in me, he is like a branch that is thrown away and withers; such branches are picked up, thrown into the fire and burned. If you remain in me and my words remain in you, ask whatever you wish, and it will be given you *(John 15:4-7)*.

"Apart from me you can do nothing." Those are strong words. They reinforce how necessary it is to stay in close relationship with God. He is the source of everything we need for life and leadership.

The key to successful leadership today is influence, not authority.
—Kenneth Blanchard

Follow my example, as I follow the example of Christ.
—1 Cor. 11:1

8

GRACE-*full* LEADERS . . .
maximize influence and minimize authority

An effective leader is not produced merely from the authority of a position or the title he or she bears. Better motivation for people to follow are influence and inspiration.

Leland Stanford founded the first transcontinental railroad that linked East to West. He was a successful rancher and landowner, a powerful man whose authority was seldom questioned. He went on to become governor of California and a U.S. senator. But his authority did not perpetuate his name; it was his influence.

Leland and Jane Stanford had one son, Leland Jr. On a European trip with his parents, young Leland contracted typhoid fever and died just a few weeks before his 16th birthday. Following his son's death, Leland Sr., then the governor of California, turned to his wife and said, "The children of California shall be our children."

Mr. and Mrs. Stanford established and endowed Stanford University as a lasting memorial to their son and as an expression of their concern for generations of young people. Leland Stanford's influence touched the world in ways his authority never could.

On a smaller scale grace-full leaders make similar choices each day. On occasion a leader must exercise his or her authority with a firm, "This is the way it will be." But if that is the overarching leadership style, there will be a negative effect on morale. Such an approach will isolate the leader from the most necessary people and can result in the best people in the organization going somewhere else.

Whenever possible, grace-full leaders seek to lead through influence rather than authority. The difference between the two approaches strikes at the heart of why and how employees/members/followers choose to respond to leadership initiatives. If the only method of motivation is the authority of the leader, the response of the follower will no doubt be a minimal commitment. The follower may comply with his hands, but not his head or heart.

How much better it is to *influence* an inner desire to participate than to *compel* participation. Grace-full leaders use influence in a number of effective ways.

Sharing Information

Influence often accompanies having the right information. Sharing important information with members of the organization creates two important results. First, it affirms to key members of the group that they are important enough to be trusted with full disclosure. Second, it creates a framework for an employee to better understand management decisions.

A couple of years ago at the university, we decided to greatly reduce the annual increase in our charges for a student's tuition and fees. Our purpose was to keep pace with our key constituents: middle-class families who found it difficult to pay for private education. Since most small private colleges are heavily tuition-dependent, a reduction in charges is immediately felt on the other side of the ledger—the funds available to pay for expenses.

Realizing that the following year would be tight financially, I had a choice to make. I could, as president of the university, use my control to declare a spending and hiring freeze. Or I could seek to influence the members of the faculty and staff to voluntarily reduce expenses as an accommodation to the university's overall strategy.

In a series of regular meetings, the members of the administrative team began to talk about our goals and the decision regarding student charges. When that decision was embraced by the university community, the climate to address spending was established. The following year, members of the faculty and staff were saying, "We can wait a while on that purchase or replacing that person." Voluntarily the entire university community worked diligently to keep expenses in line with the reduced revenue. I am convinced that this level of response and the positive morale that accompanied it would not have been possible had departmental budgets been slashed by 10 percent and compliance forced through rigid regulation of purchases.

Asking the Right Questions

It is important for a grace-full leader to remain sensitive in settings where he or she is present but not the one in charge. In my situation, I find this particularly true when I am participating in student-led meetings. I want to affirm student leadership and show a proper level of respect for student leaders, but at the same time there are situations when I want to shape the decisions being made or the methods employed.

Often the best way to introduce an alternative idea is to simply ask a question. "What would be the downside of implementing what we are talking about doing?" "Is there another way to achieve the same results while avoiding the negative response from some?" "What do you think about asking so-and-so for their reaction?" Simply asking the right questions can influence the dialogue without grabbing the reins or casting a negative shadow on the other person's leadership.

Modeling Desired Behavior

A subtle but powerful way for a leader to exert influence is by modeling the desired behavior. Leaders set the tone and express desired outcomes by what they do as well as what they say. A leader is a mentor, a template others observe.

To communicate a vision, one needs more
than words, speeches, memos,
or laminated plaques.

To communicate a vision, one needs more than words, speeches, memos, or laminated plaques. A leader must live his or her vision, day in and day out. He or she must embody the vision. People will evaluate our words by our deeds. Grace-full leaders know their actions do speak louder than words. They do not say, "Get going!" Instead their lives declare, "Let's go!" and they lead the way. Grace-full leaders do not walk behind with prod in hand; they walk beside and ahead, banner in hand, waving and leading the way.

Building Key Relationships

Influence flows through relationships. Effective leaders understand the importance of personal interaction with the key members of the organization. Leaders identify those who shape public opinion and perform strategic functions within the life of the organization. These individuals do not need an inordinate amount of attention, but a leader cannot be effective without relating to the people he or she seeks to influence.

Changing the Corporate Culture

One especially meaningful way to influence and enhance an organization is to change (or at least enrich) the corporate culture. The culture of an organization rests on the mission, values, traditions, outlook, methods, and overall spirit of the group. By adjusting any of those features, the culture is affected. To publicly celebrate the accomplishment of significant objectives is one way to do this. By affirming and being joyful about the work of others, the entire group is inspired to seek the same recognition.

Culture can also be enhanced by enabling key individuals to visit other organizations that are doing a similar work but in a different, more positive, or productive way. Observing often triggers thinking and brings into focus how a new reality might look. I have done this often with university groups and individuals. We can visit other campuses to learn ways to better perform our work.

Setting the Agenda

Set the agenda and you will have strong influence on the outcomes. Agendas are generally associated with conducting meetings, but I am using the term in a broader sense. When a leader sets the agenda for a meeting, it ensures that important items will be dealt with in the proper order and sequence. If the business of the group is restricted to the items on the agenda, the energies and resources of the group will be given to those items. But there is more to running a meeting than simply controlling the agenda. Organizations have overall corporate agendas that determine various outcomes. If the primary agenda of the group is not articulated by the leader and understood throughout the organization, lack of focus may result, or competing agendas might surface.

There is more to running a meeting than simply controlling the agenda.

The first planning initiative the university undertook after I was elected president was a multifaceted program titled "The Olivet Nazarene University *Agenda for Excellence.*" The plan identified several key objectives in each division of the university and set a time frame to accomplish those goals. We talked about it in committees, at faculty meetings, with the staff, with the Board of Trustees, and with the alumni and other stakeholders. This agenda was the focus of the president's address at the beginning of the academic year. A full-color brochure detailed the items on the agenda, and it was splashed across several of the university's official publications.

At no time, in the course of establishing the agenda, did a "decree go forth" from the president's office mandating compliance or support for these items. Yet the entire university community caught the vision, and soon the agenda became reality.

Casting a Compelling Vision

Closely related to setting the agenda is casting a compelling vision. That was certainly a big part of the *Agenda for Excellence*. Vision influences rather than mandates.

Limiting Choices

A leader can provide an opportunity for input by designing a scenario that revolves around a few preapproved choices. Perhaps you feel strongly that an individual or group should respond to a particular opportunity, problem, or challenge. However, you are hesitant to demand a specific response. Instead, try to present two or more options, and allow the person or group involved to choose among those options. This fosters a higher level of personal involvement for the group. Without being autocratic, your influence can be direct simply through limiting the choices available.

Providing Feedback

One member of your organization is working very hard, doing his or her absolute best. But in the midst of the work, that person doesn't even realize that he or she is out of step with your desires for the entire group. Putting that person back on track is imperative for your leadership to be effective. You should provide quick feedback with thoughtful evaluation in a positive manner.

When I was a boy, my father took my older brother, Michael, and me, on a shopping trip. What an adventure in the days before shopping malls and megastores! Shopping was not a routine activity for us, since we lived in a rural setting. For my father to devote the entire day to take his boys into the city was quite a deal.

The purpose for our adventure was to purchase new suits for Easter. We were a family of modest income; clothes were handed down and expected to last and be as versatile as possible. Two new suits at the same time was a special event.

When we arrived at the department store, my father affirmed us by giving us some latitude in selecting the suit we wanted. My older brother chose a very traditional blue suit, with two pairs of slacks. It was a good value, built to last, and would be appropriate for any occasion.

Next it was my turn. As my brother was selecting his suit, I had already been looking. For some reason, a rather flashy suit with large checks and bright colors caught my eye. When I announced to my dad, "Here's the one I want!" he was suddenly in an awkward position. He had the authority, the money, and the right to simply say, "You cannot have that suit. Not only would you be an embarrassment to the family dressed like that, your mother would kill me."

However, rather than breaking my spirit and questioning my judgment, he said, "Well, try it on. Let's see how you look." I didn't know it at the time, but while I was in the dressing room, my dad said to my older brother, "I don't think that suit is quite right for John, do you?" Together they hatched a plan to persuade me to choose another suit.

When I walked out, my brother took one look and covered his eyes. His feedback was not quite as subtle as my father had intended. Dad quickly responded, "Well, John, you look great. You kind of remind me of Uncle So-and-so." (He named an uncle whose judgment I had already learned to question.) Then he asked, "Do you think that suit will look all right at church?" I hadn't really been thinking about church. "I don't know, Dad; what do you think?" By this time, my brother had walked away, pretending not to know us at all.

My dad said, "Why don't you try on a couple of others before deciding." I agreed. As I modeled more traditional choices, my father's praise and my brother's return to the scene influenced me to choose a more suitable suit. The key item of influence was feedback.

Walk softly and carry a big heart
and a generous spirit.

Grace-full leadership maximizes influence and minimizes authority. Walk softly and carry a big heart and a generous spirit. Care for others as well as outcomes.

Enthusiasm is contagious. Start an epidemic.
—Don Ward

Never be lacking in zeal, but keep your spiritual fervor, serving the Lord.
—Rom. 12:11

9

GRACE-*full* LEADERS . . .
are passionate

During one of his early travels, Sigmund Freud visited the lovely church of San Pietro in Rome and came face-to-face with Michelangelo's statue of Moses. Years later, still gripped by that experience, he returned to the church and, day after day over a three-week period, studied the statue, measured it, sketched it, and lingered for hours over its detail. He noted how precisely Moses held the tablets against his side; how he turned his cold, stern face toward those who were worshiping the golden calf; and how his long beard flowed to one side. Freud was taken by the way Michelangelo had captured the passion of Moses. He saw in the statue not a passion unleashed impulsively, but a passion under control that gave strength, determination, and direction.

A few days after I was elected as a university president, two friends gave me a beautiful porcelain replica of that statue. It stands in my office just beyond my desk. I see it nearly every day and have never grown tired of it. It is a great symbol of passionate leadership—a passion born of conviction that clearly identified Moses as the leader.

Moses was one of the first towering charismatic leaders who influenced history in two ways: through his personality and through the ideals for which he stood. Moses combined both the power of his presence and the passion of his character.

There is a passionate dimension to grace-full leadership. In a way, to lead is to lay your life on the line—your time, energies, resources, and reputation. It is all out or get out. For a leader, it is more than just a job. This dimension of leadership fills the leader with desire and commitment.

Passion takes many forms. Sometimes it fills our work with great energy and a sense of adventure. The mythic figure named Odysseus (also known by the Latin name Ulysses) is a symbol of the hero adventurer, the knight, the pilgrim, the pioneer, the explorer. He set out with his men on the high seas to visit strange lands, meeting in his adventures various human and mythological creatures, each with a threat to offer and each with a lesson to teach.

No two days were ever the same for Odysseus, and he had to use his strength and wit to face the full array of human temptations and trials. In the face of it all he had to sail on. Just so, a leader must dream, must be able to see the eternal in the ordinary while possessing boldness and fortitude. Grace-full leadership is not an approach for the weak or lazy. It is not found at the end of the road marked "least resistance."

Alfred Lord Tennyson wrote a dramatic monologue about Ulysses, describing him as an old man remembering his journeys, thinking of who he had been and where he had been. In the monologue, the aging Ulysses determines to set out again, to set sail once more, to keep exploring and learning and striving to the end. Some of Tennyson's lines read:

> *Come, my friends.*
> *'Tis not too late to seek a newer world.*
> *Push off, and sitting well in order smite*
> *The sounding furrows; for my purpose holds*
> *To sail beyond the sunset, and the baths*
> *Of all the western stars, until I die.*
> *It may be that gulfs will wash us down;*
> *It may be we shall touch the Happy Isles,*
> *And see the great Achilles, whom we knew.*
> *Though much is taken, much abides; and though*
> *We are not now that strength which in old days*
> *Moved earth and heaven, that which we are, we are—*
> *One equal temper of heroic hearts,*
> *Made weak by time and fate, but strong in will*
> *To strive, to seek, to find, and not to yield.*

"One equal temper of heroic hearts, / . . . strong in will / To strive, to seek, to find, and not to yield." How stirring! That is passion, and that is the spirit of all who make the journey of leadership.

Another mythological figure, named Sisyphus, shows a different side of passion. Sisyphus was the legendary king of ancient Corinth. He was condemned to push a great stone tediously up a great hill, only to have it slip from his grasp just as it reached the crest and then to roll down the hill again. Time after time he would garner his strength and start over: his back aching, his muscles straining, his body sweating, only to have the stone escape his control each time just before he reached the top.

Again and again Sisyphus stood bewildered and dejected, and yet each time he wearily pulled together his resources and his resolve to try once again. Albert Camus, the French writer, wrote a philosophical essay in 1942 called "The Myth of Sisyphus." Though he was an ancient character, Camus suggested that Sisyphus was a symbol of modern man and of life in an age where many persistently labor but feel that their labor has no ultimate meaning, that there is no success at the end of the day.

The tiresomeness of the routine must be overcome with a passion for what lies beyond the work itself.

Sisyphus represents a type of hopeless heroism, a kind of fruitless valor. But this mythic figure can indeed serve as a model for leaders. There is a certain drudgery and endlessness to work in general and to leadership in particular. The tiresomeness of the routine must be overcome with a passion for what lies beyond the work itself. How tough it is to push our rocks up our hills day after day, not knowing why and never reaching the top, always struggling and straining and stretching, always starting over.

Grace-full leaders must have something of Sisyphus's tenacity and perseverance. Just as they must have the courage and energy of Odysseus, so, too, leaders must have the perseverance and determination of Sisyphus. We would like for all our work to be exciting and immediately rewarding, but it isn't always that way; much of life and labor is tough and boring and routine, and therein lies the challenge to excellence.

Our challenge is to resist the strain of seeing each day as "just one more day" or each task of leadership as simply "one more" in an endless series of tasks. It is vital that a leader resists the self-talk of defeat. "I did this yesterday and the day before and the day before that. What difference will it make what kind of job I do?" Excellence comes as we overcome the dailiness of our work and mission. Excellence comes inch by inch and day by day. It comes as we work through the tedium, doing our best at every point time after time.

○══╪══○

> *In the final analysis grace-full*
> *leadership is an expression of*
> *commitment to Christ.*

○══╪══○

A third figure, not from mythology but from history itself, shows us another side of passionate leadership. His name is Jesus.

Jesus could have lived His life in a small village. He could have had the comforts of home. He could have lived to a ripe old age. He could have settled for popularity. But a fire burned within Him. A mission compelled Him, and so He gave himself away. He "went about doing good" (Acts 10:38, KJV) and saying to all who would hear and heed, "Come, follow me."

God's cause can bring passion to any odyssey. In the final analysis grace-full leadership is an expression of commitment to Christ. The daily routines of life can become flooded with eternal meaning. The presence and blessing of Jesus can transform the ordinary tedium into magnificent service.

Grace-full leaders are passionate about their cause.

A leader who is not passionately committed to the mission and cause of the organization will find it hard to go the second mile and do the difficult items often required of leaders. Without passion, leaders will find it difficult to inspire commitment from others. However, when passion is present, there is added power. Passion brings energy and galvanizes support from others. "The world will make way for someone who knows what he or she wants, because there is not much competition when it comes to passionate commitment."[1]

Grace-full leaders are passionate about the people they serve and with whom they serve.

All leadership takes place within the context of human relationship. Leaders must care deeply about the people with whom they work. When people in the organization are convinced that the leader cares about them, they feel significant. They rightly believe that what they do makes a difference, and therefore, they feel empowered and become more passionate about their individual work.

In organizations where people are valued, community and teamwork develop, and those forces help create and sustain corporate morale. Passionate leadership affects people and results in fun, stimulating, and challenging work. This identification, in turn, fosters the desire to be part of the team. When others are counting on your input, there is added power and purpose.

Jack Welch, CEO of General Electric, said it boldly when he suggested that the future will "not belong to 'managers' or those who can make the numbers dance. The world will belong to the passionate, driven leaders—people who not only have enormous amounts of energy but who can also energize those whom they lead."[2] Passion is contagious, and a leader's influence can spark passion and commitment from colleagues and coworkers.

Grace-full leaders are passionate about the One who calls individuals into leadership.

All grace-full leaders recognize the hand of God at work in their lives. They see their leadership as an extension of God's grace and His kingdom. Their commitment to Christ must be complete, nothing held back, nothing reserved.

This is particularly true for leaders in the church. The vitality of the church does not depend on elaborate organization or creative administration, important as those are; not even on eloquent preaching or adequate theology, valuable as they are; or on unlimited financial resources, helpful though they may be. What the church needs now, as always, is a band of men and women who care more about God and His precious kingdom than anything else on earth. We need a multitude of men and women "press[ing] on toward the goal to win the prize for which God has called" them (Phil. 3:14), taking hold of that for which He took hold of us.[3] "The church which pitches its tents without looking out constantly for new horizons, which does not continually strike camp, is being untrue to its calling."[4]

For grace-full leaders merely to repeat Jesus' words is not to continue His work; they must be intent on reproducing His life and passion. Such leaders are not building their kingdoms, but His. Grace-full leaders are passionate people, set aflame by the Spirit.

The challenge is to be a light, not a judge; to be a model, not a critic.
—Stephen R. Covey

I am among you as one who serves.
—Luke 22:27

10

GRACE-*full* LEADERS . . .
focus primarily on the body, not the head

The ultimate goal of understanding leadership is not to produce great or charismatic leaders but to enhance the life and effectiveness of the organization. The measure of leadership is not the quality of the head, but the tone of the body. "The signs of outstanding leadership appear primarily among the followers."[1]

Therefore, the mind of a grace-full leader questions, "Is this organization or group healthy and productive?" "Leadership is a concept of owing certain things to the institution. It is a way of thinking about institutional heirs, a way of thinking about stewardship as contrasted with ownership."[2]

The university where I serve as president does not belong to me. It is entrusted to me for this time, and, thus, the ultimate measure of my leadership will be the quality of the institution when I leave. This shift from self-focused leadership to thinking and working solely for the good of the institution takes grace. It is the grace of service.

Clyde Cook, longtime president of Biola University, wrote: "I am the temporary office holder of the presidency of Biola University. It would be easy to become enamored with self and feel that I am 'Mr. Biola,' and that the whole organization revolves around me. This is a deadly perception, as the organization can function quite well without me. There have been other presidents before me, and there will be other presidents after me until the Lord returns, so it behooves me to hold the office lightly and to realize that it is temporary."[3]

Dr. Cook's counsel about holding one's leadership lightly is a challenge made possible by grace. Grace teaches us that even leadership is a gift and that everyone serves, ultimately, by God's providential leadership.

Before satisfying your own needs as a leader, look first to the needs of the organization and individuals who are a part of it. The real test is not the leader's personal success but the health of the organization and the success of the men and women within it. This perspective is not natural, but it is powerful. It sets a tone and provides an example for how others should respond. To focus on the body rather than on the head means that the leader is the ultimate servant of the organization.

John 13 shows us a beautiful example of this focus on service. In a meeting/dining room in the ancient city of Jerusalem, Jesus is gathering with His disciples. Imagine you are in this Upper Room behind a special pane of glass. You can see and hear what goes on, but no one can see you. The room is empty, and it is the evening of the Last Supper, the night before Jesus' death. The custom of the day would provide a servant at the door to wash the guests' feet as they arrive for the Passover meal. However, as you look around the room, you see the bowl, a pitcher of water, and the towel—but no servant.

Standing quietly behind the glass, you begin to hear voices. It is Jesus and the Twelve. The first disciple walks in the door and looks for the servant, but there is no one there. Decision time. Does he wash his own feet? Does he take off his garment and become a servant himself? What will he do? He looks at the table and tries to decide where Jesus is going to sit, and he moves quickly to take the best spot. He wants a prominent position.

A second disciple enters and sizes up the situation: no servant. He says to himself, "Well, if the first guy isn't going to do anything, I'm not going to. I'm as good as he is." One by one they file in, walk right by the water basin, and take their places, with their feet in each other's faces.

The last to arrive is Jesus. You see Him standing for a moment at the door. He, too, sizes up the situation. Watch Him. He looks at the water; He looks at the unwashed feet of the disciples. You can see it in His eyes. Time after time He has poured out His heart to these men regarding the dangers of a "me first" mind-set. Time after time He has talked to them about serving rather than being served.

But there is not one of them willing to wash the others' feet. And what is worse, not one of the brothers is even humble enough to come forward as Jesus enters. They won't even do it for Him.

Watch closely now. Jesus walks to the table, sits with His disciples for a moment, then gets up from the table. The others are talking and preoccupied. You keep your eyes on Jesus, shifting your weight a little to see Him better.

He moves toward the doorway and stands by the basin for a moment. Then, without ceremony, He begins to take off His outer garment. He girds himself with a towel just as an ordinary servant would do. As He pours the water from the pitcher to the basin, the room grows quiet and still.

Looking into the eyes of the disciples, you first see bewilderment ("What is He doing?"), then disbelief, then embarrassment. As Jesus comes to the first of the disciples to begin this foot washing, what do you see—agony, regret, perhaps even tears?

It is as if each disciple is saying, "What's the matter with me? Although I am a follower of Jesus, I am still preoccupied with myself. My whole world revolves around my self-interest. How could I have done this? It's one thing not to have washed the feet of my brothers, whom I love, but I wouldn't even wash the feet of my Savior. How could I have missed it?"

Jesus works His way around the room. Peter resists for a minute, but then cooperates. When Jesus finishes, He puts the basin back and lays the towel aside, puts on His robe, returns to the table, and says to them, "Do you understand what I have done for you? . . . Now that I, your Lord and Teacher, have washed your feet, you also should wash one another's feet. I have set you an example that you should do as I have done" (John 13:12, 14-15).

The relationship of the leader to the follower is like a marriage.

The example is clear. The leader should create an environment that focuses on the needs of others rather than the needs of the leader. One benefit of such an environment is that employees and coworkers become more committed to the organization.

Commitment is a two-way street. In a way, the relationship of the leader to the follower is like a marriage. If both partners look out only for their own needs, desires, and rights, the quality of the relationship is greatly diminished. But if each has the other's interest at heart, both prosper and flourish. So care for the folks you work with.

William Pollard, chairman of ServiceMaster, lists the following as "immutables of our firm."

- Truth cannot be compromised.
- Everyone has a job to do, and no one should benefit at the expense of another.
- We should treat everyone with dignity and worth.
- Our combined efforts are for the benefit of our owners, members, and customers, and not for some select group.
- We must always be willing to serve.[4]

These characteristics are focused on the good of the body. From time to time, every person in an organization needs support, training, encouragement, and nurture. One of the leader's responsibilities is to see that this happens. The Bible underscores the worth of every individual and the value (and necessity) of serving others. This biblical teaching provides the appropriate tone for leadership, and grace provides the spiritual energy to make it possible.

Focusing on the body rather than the head makes a difference in how a leader responds to criticism. If you are concerned only about your ego or how you will look in a given situation, then your response to criticism will probably be defensive and personal. But if your focus is on the welfare of others first, then you are better armed to respond appropriately when criticism comes—and criticism *will* come to anyone in leadership.

The wise leader knows that criticism is simply a part of organizational and institutional life, and therefore he or she does not personalize it or seek to respond in a way that hurts others. The

"I'll show you . . ." or "If you want to be that way about it . . ." attitude is not the response of a grace-filled leader.

Leadership focus is vital. If you look only at how a decision benefits you instead of what is ultimately good for all, you will fail to care first for the body. Grace provides the lens through which to see a new possibility.

Tom Chappell, president of Tom's of Maine, suggests that part of a leader's role is to help the company become community.[5] Community is more than just geographic boundaries. There are facets of community, beyond location, that shape the character and ethos of a company or organization.

For the most part, an organization is, in some ways, a collection of communities. Often there are departments within divisions of the company. There may even be various buildings or locations where different groups of individuals work. The organization is part of some local community and a member of the *business community* in that area.

⊶

Community within the workplace is worth nurturing, for it nurtures and sustains those who work together.

⊶

Community within a company may be as narrow as one office, one row of machinery, or one table in the break room. Yet it may also be, at the same moment, as wide as the world itself through an extended web of international relationships. Community within the workplace is worth nurturing, for it nurtures and sustains those who work together. When and where a genuine spirit of community thrives, it creates better people and enriches the work of those involved. Community brings about a synergy that results in the whole being much more than the sum of the parts.

It is no small thing for a group of 3 or 300 individuals to work together, elbow to elbow, day after day. That's about all the "community" one can take sometimes, isn't it? But this is the very crucible that produces character and citizenship while enriching the work experience and personal life of those involved.

A spirit of community doesn't just happen; it must be fashioned and fostered, nourished and maintained. Community can be a fragile thing in many ways. Relationships can be broken, isolation can set in, and communication can dissipate. Employees and coworkers can drift apart, living in their own little worlds, almost untouched by the others.

If there is to be genuine community within an organization, the people who work together must become more than a collection of individuals associated only through job descriptions, work orders, and business plans. The grace-full leader finds a way for each one to be part of *one* community—a multifaceted community, yes, but a community nonetheless.

How is that possible? Sociologists tell us that community starts as individuals begin to share a common ground. Generally that means geographic ground; but while most groups do share a defined location, there is another kind of *common ground* that unites people into community—the common ground of shared values and mission. It takes more than just a company logo to give identity to a group. Values, priorities, and traditions shape the words and deeds that color the people who are in contact each day.

In all areas the guiding principle and pathway of community must be the Lord's great commandment. Jesus instructs us to "love the Lord your God with all your heart and with all your soul and with all your mind" and to "love your neighbor as yourself" (Matt. 22:37, 39). At the heart of this commandment is a simple value of and respect for one another.

How do we build community? We demonstrate the love of God to employees, colleagues, and all others with whom we have contact. We must embody an attitude of service and a willingness to invest ourselves in the lives of one another. Jesus shared the parable of the Good Samaritan to reinforce this teaching. That story reminds us that our neighbor is anyone in need. This is the test of love—the measure of community.

A company or organization ought to be more than just a place to work, more than just a set of buildings or a catalog of products and services. A business can become, by God's holy grace, a community where employees "carry each other's burdens, and in this way . . . fulfill the law of Christ" (Gal. 6:2).

— SECTION TWO —

The Traits of Grace-Full Leaders

Grace-full leaders . . .

- understand accountability
- interact rather than react
- follow their "knows"
- are willing to follow as well as lead
- maintain their balance
- have double vision
- "go deep"
- are skilled meteorologists
- anticipate through planning, pathfinding, planting, and prospecting
- take care

There is no such thing as a minor lapse of integrity.
—Tom Peters

Jesus told his disciples: "There was a rich man whose manager was accused
of wasting his possessions. So he called him in and asked him,
'What is this I hear about you? Give an account of your management,
because you cannot be manager any longer.'"
—Luke 16:1-2

11
GRACE-*full* LEADERS . . .
understand accountability

Accountability is a two-way street. To lead effectively means holding others accountable; to be a leader means holding yourself accountable. "Being accountable is a ledger of promises made and promises kept."[1] Leaders are accountable not only to the hierarchical structure but also to the people with whom they work.

The climate in our society has slowly but surely eroded accountability for words and actions. Leaders must be aware of this current and develop a strong sense of personal accountability. Grace-full leaders must practice what they preach.

Embracing accountability means being open to assessment and evaluation by others. Listening openly to candid feedback is a pathway to improvement and respect. Leaders who manage and monitor others must first manage and monitor themselves. "Our stewardship and servanthood will be called into accountability before God, not just on judgment day, but every day; and especially in those moments when our leadership is put on the line by personal temptations and pivotal decisions."[2]

Personal accountability is a function of character, and character is a prime ingredient of leadership. During the Whitewater and Monica Lewinsky events, the majority of the American public decided that as long as President Bill Clinton did his job well, then his personal life did not matter. However, that is not the case for leaders who follow Christ. Theirs is a higher calling that can only be fulfilled through God's grace.

Grace-full leaders live a public life and are held to a high level of accountability both within and beyond the organization. It takes a high level of integrity to pass the test of accountability. "In times of constant change, it's easy for people to think that even the fundamental laws governing human decency and behavior have changed. But they haven't."[3]

The consistent demonstration of integrity is essential to grace-full leadership. Followers and colleagues must be wholeheartedly convinced of their leader's integrity, and integrity finds its roots in one's basic character.

*Character is the moral code
of personhood.*

In Robert Wilson's *Character Above All*, a book of biographical essays about 10 U.S. presidents, Peggy Noonan makes this observation: "In a president, character is everything. A president doesn't have to be brilliant; . . . he doesn't have to be clever; you can hire clever. You can hire pragmatic, and you can buy and bring in policy wonks. But you can't buy courage and decency, you can't rent a strong moral sense."[4]

What she observes about the presidency is true of all men and women: "character is everything." Character is the moral code of personhood. It involves integrity, honesty, patience, courage, kindness, generosity, and a strong sense of personal responsibility. Too much of the success and human relations literature of the past has been personality-oriented when it should have been character-based. But character ultimately forms the foundation of personality, and character often determines our success or failure as a leader.

Just as a beautiful house built upon a poor foundation cannot provide a stable and secure habitation, neither can a veneer of personality cover or compensate for weak character. "In the end, your integrity is all you've got."[5]

Solomon said it wisely in Prov. 4:23: "Above all else, guard your heart, for it is the wellspring of life."

Notice that this is a command, an imperative, particularly for those in leadership. The language and imagery here is quite descriptive. There are two word pictures suggested by this phrase, "guard your heart."

The first is a military image, where a commander posts a sentinel to watch and protect. There is the perception of danger for anything left unguarded. There is the imagery of an enemy who seeks to do harm unless we are watchful. So as a soldier might do, leaders should also stand guard over their hearts and actions.

The second image is the picture of someone who has a great treasure to protect. In the Bible, the heart is the center of personal being. It is not merely the home of the affections, but also the seat of the will and of moral purpose. We are to guard our hearts more carefully than we guard anything else.

Think about the elaborate security methods developed to guard our possessions. Like many folks, I drive a car with a built-in security system. When it is bumped or if someone tries to pry open a door or window, the horn sounds and the lights flash. The attention of everyone for blocks is drawn immediately to that car. As far as I know, the only time this alarm system has gone off was one night just as I climbed into the car in the Wal-Mart parking lot. Somehow, the alarm system was triggered, and suddenly the horn began to blow, the lights began to flash, and a crowd gathered around to point and stare. Then the security guard, who regularly drives through the parking lot, came roaring up behind me. I would have been happy to give the car away.

We put such elaborate energy and resources into guarding that which rusts and decays and that which can be stolen. How much more important it is to guard our integrity and reputation in leadership.

The Scripture gives us some counsel concerning the "how" of guarding our hearts. For example:

- "I have hidden your word in my heart that I might not sin against you" (Ps. 119:11).
- "I seek you with all my heart; do not let me stray from your commands" (Ps. 119:10).
- "Turn my heart toward your statutes and not toward selfish gain" (Ps. 119:36).
- "Teach me your way, O LORD, and I will walk in your truth; give me an undivided heart, that I may fear your name" (Ps. 86:11).
- "Trust in the LORD with all your heart and lean not on your own understanding" (Prov. 3:5).

We must be careful about what we treasure, for as Jesus said, "Where your treasure is, there your heart will be also" (Matt. 6:21).

Bob Benson wrote:

> Spring is here—the young are smitten with love,
> the ground is covered with greenery,
> and the garage is bursting with junk.
>
> Where did it all come from—and where is it all going?
>
> With the advent of cleaning time, attics everywhere are
> "crowdedly testifying" that as human beings
> we are accumulators, collectors, junk dealers.
>
> And our assortment of goods—
> whether it be hats, houses,
> clothes, cameras, furniture, lamps—
> the Master called our treasure.
>
> He didn't call it treasure because of its usefulness—
> lovely chairs, minus one leg,
> lots of jars—without tops,
> magazines old enough to be in a barber shop.
> And not because of its value
> did He call it treasure.
> They'd charge you to haul it off.
>
> But treasure, He said,
> because they are pictures of
> places where you put
> your heart for awhile.

They were all things you could not do without,
        that you just had to have.
Remember the day you signed the notes,
        the painful monthly payments
to buy this collection of things
        you no longer use?

They were treasures then,
        but just like He said—
                moths and time,
        rust and the kids,
thieves and the dog have
reduced them to spring cleaning
                projects.
Basements, attics, carports, dormitory rooms—
        eloquently echoing the
timeless words of the Master:

"Be careful what you treasure—
        for where your treasure is
                your heart will be."[6]

"Guard your heart," the passage says. Put a sentinel on duty.
Watch it carefully. Protect it. Pay attention to it. Keep it clean.
Clear away the debris. This is a command.

And there is an intense priority here: "Above all else." Many
things in life are optional; we may take them or leave them.
There are things that have value if you have time to pursue
them. In fact, much of the success of life is learning to make
those kinds of choices. If you cannot do all things, then what ba-
sis should you use to decide to do certain things?

⊶⊷

To remember God and our
ultimate accountability to Him
is life's highest priority.

⊶⊷

In his classic novel *One Hundred Years of Solitude,* Colombian author Gabriel Garcia Marquez tells of a village where people were afflicted with a strange plague of forgetfulness. It was a kind of contagious amnesia. Moving slowly through the population of the village, the plague caused people to forget the names of even the most common everyday objects.

One young man, yet unaffected, tried to limit the damage by putting labels on everything. "This is a table." "This is a window." "This is a cow; it has to be milked every morning." And at the entrance to the town, on the main road, he put up two large signs. One read, "The name of our village is Macondo." And the other sign, the largest sign of all, read, "God exists."

Above all else, the thing he wanted to be sure to remember and to help others remember was that God exists. Perhaps, in the course of time, we as leaders may forget much of what we have learned. We may forget dates and places, names and faces—and all of that forgetting may not matter too much.

But if we forget God, if we forget the One to whom we belong, if our hearts get cluttered and crowded and cramped, if we lose our way spiritually, then no other amount of remembering will make much difference. To remember God and our ultimate accountability to Him is life's highest priority, and so "above all else, guard your heart."

In the film *Chariots of Fire*, the master of Caius College greets the first-year students with these words: "Let me exhort you, let each of you discover where your true chance of greatness lies. . . . Seize this chance, rejoice in it, and let no power or persuasion deter you in your task."[7]

This is good advice: sift through the many options in life, and choose the one that fits you best; then give yourself wholeheartedly to it. Scripture teaches us that in a life filled with many options, there are some overriding principles not optional, and those must take precedence. This is such a case, and the writer gives the reason why: "Guard your heart, for it is the wellspring of life."

Every person has an inner being, a center from which all of life flows. Therefore our thoughts, deeds, and attitudes are all outward manifestations of this inner self, the heart; and supreme care should be directed there. When the heart is pure, all that flows from it will be pure; but if the heart becomes bitter or sour or soiled, that which flows forth will also be bitter and sour and soiled. Life is lived inside out.

The world around us reverses that formula. People might think that if we have the right things on the outside—the right clothes, friends, possessions, and positions—then the inside will be happy and at peace. But that is not true, for the wellspring of life is from within, not without.

King David prayed it well, as he said, "Create in me a pure heart, O God, and renew a steadfast spirit within me" (Ps. 51:10). David had it all: money, sex, power. But everything was not enough without God. If leaders are to be all that God has created and gifted them to be, they must begin within.

What comes to mind when you hear or see the word *saunter*? Do you picture a leisurely stroll through the mall, a walk in the park, an amble across the campus? *Saunter* is a pleasant word, a word of leisure. No hurry, no worries—just out for a walk in any direction.

The word *saunter*, however, has an interesting history. It is derived from the French words *saincte terre*, meaning "Holy Land." During the period of the great Crusades, soldiers marched across Europe on their way to liberate the Holy Land, the *saincte terre*.

As these individuals journeyed through France, Christians who lived along the main roads and in the towns and villages would often give these travelers food and accommodation for the night as they continued on their "holy journey."

Well, it didn't take long for some people to learn that they could *pretend* to be going *à la saincte terre* (to the Holy Land). They had no real intention to go there but found this was a convenient way to get a free night's room and board—to travel from place to place at will and be received with honor, respect, and hospitality.

After a time, these impostors became identified and were called "saunterers": those who pretended to be going somewhere, those who appeared to be on a holy journey, but who were, in fact, impostors. Here were individuals who professed what they did not really possess and pretended to be what they were not.

❦

Leaders must guard against the influence of the culture of ease that surrounds us.

❦

Leaders must guard against the influence of the culture of ease that surrounds us. A lack of accountability on the part of some leaders may cause them, like those early saunterers, to follow Christ for what is to be gained rather than what they may give to His cause.

Accountability means that leaders take responsibility for their words and actions. And just as one is accountable *to* others, the grace-full leader is also accountable *for* others. Leaders must bear a sense of responsibility for the individuals with whom and for whom they work. Leaders often are called upon to balance the needs of people and of the institution.

Learn to lead, not contain.
—Frances Hesselbein

The prudent see danger and take refuge.
—Prov. 27:12

12

GRACE-*full* LEADERS . . .
interact rather than react

It all began in a small barn on a side street in a residential area away from the central city. At approximately 8:15 on the evening of Sunday, October 8, 1871, smoke first appeared coming from the Patrick O'Leary barn at 137 DeKovan Street.

Whether a cow actually kicked over a lantern is a matter of conjecture; whatever the cause, Chicago, that night, was a disaster waiting to happen. Chicago was a boomtown if there ever was one. In just 50 years it had grown to become the largest city in the West. Its population stood at 334,000, making it second only to New York City.

Buildings had shot up like spring weeds. The construction was shabby at best. The *Chicago Tribune*, only a month before the fire, noted that bricks and cornicing from several buildings fell daily into the streets, endangering pedestrians.

Away from downtown, Chicago was little more than a massive shantytown of hastily constructed, wooden structures. The O'Leary house was located in one such area—a working-class neighborhood not far from the stockyards and sawmills of the southwest side.

The summer and fall of 1871 had been particularly dry. It was now October, and only two and a half inches of rain had fallen since the Fourth of July. There were fires often in the city; and in fact, on the day before the great fire, four entire city blocks of the town had burned to the ground.

Matthias Schaffer, a watchman on duty at the courthouse downtown, first noticed smoke from the O'Leary barn, several miles away. He sounded the alarm at box 342. Then, like the watchman on the *Titanic* who first noticed the iceberg, Schaffer could only watch with fright as tragedy loomed before him.

The flames grew higher and higher. By 10:30 the fire was completely out of control, and the die of disaster was cast. A stiff wind from the southwest pushed the flames toward downtown, ironically sparing the O'Leary residence from any damage.

The flames leaped from house to house, then block to block, and finally from one bank of the Chicago River to the other. The firestorm caused great wind channels that helped topple stone buildings in the fire's path.

The streets were soon filled with people fleeing with whatever belongings they could carry. One eyewitness account, for example, mentioned that an undertaker and his assistants were seen fleeing with their stock of coffins raised above their heads—a grim harbinger of the danger at hand.

And the noise was terrific. To the roar of the fire was added the crash of falling buildings and the constant explosions of combustibles. To these were added the cries of desperate, frightened people. People trapped on upper floors were forced to leap for safety, many of them suffering severe injury.

The great number of vagrants in the city became an army of looters raiding at the fringes of the firewall. When the prisoners were released from the holding cells of the city, they quickly joined the bandit brigade.

The fire continued to burn throughout the night and all the next day. The Chicago Fire was one of the greatest urban disasters in the history of our country. It raged unchecked for two days, consuming nearly everything in its path. The flames shot hundreds of feet into the air, and the orange glow could be seen from several states.

Early Tuesday morning, a rain began to blanket the city. Eventually the fire halted, but not before it had burned its way to the lake and then northward to Lincoln Park.

On Wednesday, into the smoking, smoldering city came the National Guard under the command of Civil War hero Gen. Philip Sheridan. Martial law was established, and an assessment of the damage was begun.

The destruction was almost beyond calculation. The fire had destroyed 18,000 buildings. Only 6 buildings were left standing in an area of 2,100 acres. Most of the city's residents were left homeless in the wake of the Great Chicago Fire.

A grace-full leader must be able to effectively assess both the challenges and opportunities that constantly face organizations.

This story of the Chicago Fire illustrates some of the basic principles of leadership, particularly when an organization faces an uncertain and ever-changing environment. A grace-full leader must be able to effectively assess both the challenges and opportunities that constantly face organizations. In response to these the leader must choose to be either inactive, reactive, proactive, or interactive. What you choose among these four responses reflects what you believe about yourself as well as the environment in which you lead.

1. The first response is to be *inactive.*

In this situation the leader probably has a negative image of the environment and a poor self-image. This is the person who says, "I can't change what happens around me. I have no control over what may or may not affect my business or organization."

It's called management by crossing your fingers. The inactive leader simply takes life as it comes. This is certainly the exception, for most people in business know that you cannot survive long by being inactive.

On the night of the great blaze, word of what was happening spread like the fire itself throughout the city. A large crowd gathered on the north side of the Chicago River to watch the south side of the city as it burned. These folks did not realize that such a fire could easily leap from one side of the water to the other. So they simply just stood and watched, foolishly assuming that their homes and businesses were safe. "It might happen to others, but not me" was their attitude. They were frozen with inactivity until the fire began to literally rain down upon them. In that moment they quickly moved from being inactive to the second response.

2. A second response is to be *reactive.*

The reactive leader is negative about the environment but positive about his or her own efforts. This person says, "I cannot do anything about the environment. I can't make the fire go away, but once it gets to me, I'll do my best to put it out."

There are some leaders who spend much of their time just putting out fires. Sometimes they win, sometimes they lose. But this constant fire fighting, this tyranny of the urgent, takes them away from many of the real issues related to staying in business and being successful.

3. A third and better response is to be *proactive*.

The proactive person is positive about both the environment and about himself or herself. The self-talk here is this: "I can help create the right business environment, or I can overcome this obstacle if I take the initiative."

There were a few folks on that night of terror in Chicago who, upon hearing of the fire long before it reached them, even long before they knew for sure that it would reach them, immediately began to take proactive steps.

They loaded wagons and emptied stores and warehouses as best they could. They immediately began soaking down their businesses and homes with water carried from the lake. They even set a few small fires to create a firebreak if possible. Unfortunately, the magnitude of that disaster was such that most of these efforts had little effect, apart from those who could move their belongings. Nonetheless, it was the right response.

4. One other possibility, if you're not inactive or reactive or even proactive, is to be *interactive*.

Like the person who is proactive, this individual is positive concerning both the environment as well as his or her business. But there is an added dimension of a deeper recognition, not only that a leader can proactively affect the surrounding environment, but also that the environment can shape the leader. This happens in negative ways that elicit a more immediate reaction and positive ways that open opportunities for new ventures and creative partnerships with others whose businesses and organizations may be facing many of the same pressures. The interactive leader says this: "What I do proactively must be a result of what I learn reactively from the changing world around me."

This concept of interactive leadership rests on two observations.

a. As much as we would like to put everything neatly into well-defined pigeonholes, real life is not that way. People function at different times in different ways. While we may have a dominant style, inactive or reactive or proactive, we do different things at different times.

For example, while I am generally proactive in my leadership at the university, I do spend some of my time putting out fires. If I don't, those small fires will become firestorms. And there are times when I choose to be inactive. I simply don't respond; I judge that it may be too soon to act, or I may not yet know how to proactively address a given concern. This leads me to the second observation, which is the issue of timing.

b. Think again about the fire. The basic difference among the inactive, reactive, and the proactive responses was timing. The inactive people did nothing. The reactors misread the danger and thus did not act until the fire reached their homes or businesses. The proactive folks began to respond long before they smelled the smoke. All made different choices regarding the fire, and each was basically a time choice.

Interactive leadership is a recognition that we may legitimately act in different ways at different times, depending on the interaction we have with the circumstances confronting us. Management is both a science and an art. This is the art part. It is a way to maximize our timing and to learn from the environment as we plan our proactive and reactive responses.

In the book titled *Leadership Jazz* by Max DePree, I was pleased to find his description of this very concept but with an entirely different vocabulary:

> I enjoy jazz, and one way to think about leadership is to consider a jazz band. Jazz-band leaders must choose the music, find the right musicians, and perform—in public. But the effect of the performance depends on so many things—the environment, the musicians, the need for everyone to perform both as individuals and as a group, the absolute dependence of the leader on the members of the band and the members upon the leader. What a summary of an organization. . . . We have much to learn from jazz-band leaders, for jazz, like leadership, combines the unpredictability of the future with the gifts of individuals.[1]

One example of interactive leadership from my work is the observations made in the last decade of the dramatic change in the environment of higher education. Among the many changes was the emergence of the adult learner. When people think of college, they normally think of the person between 18 and 22. But now the *average* age of individuals taking university level work is nearly 27, which means that there are many students enrolled in some form of university level education who are much older than the traditional 18-22 group.

Facing a decline in the pool of 18- to 22-year-olds, the inactive college just keeps doing what they have done for years, and enrollment falls. The reactive school says, "We must work harder," and they double their efforts to attract the traditional student. They may have some short-term success, but the pressure is great, and the short-term success is difficult to sustain. The proactive leader spots the trend early and begins to add new programs and expands the curriculum in order to attract the new adult learner.

In addition to some reactive and proactive responses, the university where I work has taken an interactive approach by forming partnerships that could capitalize on the very changes that challenged our enrollment. This means that our plans are formed by the ways in which the environment affects us.

○━✦━○

Grace-full leaders understand that
choosing the right response often calls for
wisdom beyond just the facts and figures
of a given situation.

○━✦━○

We developed degree completion programs geared toward the older adult who had begun college but who had not yet finished. We expanded our graduate school. We began to actively reach out to the community college graduates and target certain geographic markets. As a result, the university has experienced steady growth and development in nearly every area.

Grace-full leaders understand that choosing the right response often calls for wisdom beyond just the facts and figures of a given situation and for faith to lead when challenge comes. Faith and wisdom—both of these are gifts of the Spirit. While grace-full leaders are far from infallible, they do have the spiritual resources to augment their natural gifts and experiences and are thus able to interact with confidence rather than simply react from fear.

Correct principles are like compasses: they are always pointing the way.
And if we know how to read them, we won't get lost, confused,
or fooled by conflicting voices and values.
—Stephen R. Covey

The quiet words of the wise are more to be heeded
than the shouts of a ruler of fools.
—Eccles. 9:17

13

GRACE-*full* LEADERS . . .
follow their "knows"

Just as the Great Revolution was getting under way in Russia, a rabbi on his way to the synagogue was stopped at gunpoint by a soldier. With his rifle pointed directly at the rabbi, the soldier said in a gruff voice, "Who are you, and what are you doing here?"

The rabbi replied with a question of his own: "How much do they pay you for doing this job?"

The soldier replied, "Twenty kopecks."

Then the rabbi said, "I will pay you twenty-five kopecks if every day you stop me right here and ask me those two questions."[1]

If a leader knows the answer to those two questions, "Who are you?" and "What are you doing here?" all else will follow in good time and good measure. Albert Einstein was once asked what was really vital in mathematics. He stepped to the chalkboard and erased a board full of equations and then wrote 2 plus 2 equals 4. "That's what's really vital in math," he replied. The most intricate and complicated formulas and problems of math are hopeless without a foundation upon which you can rely. So it is with life, faith, and leadership.

How to attain and evaluate what you need to know in order to make the right decision or cast the appropriate vision is a vital component of leadership. Knowing is both an art and a science, both a technique and an instinct.

Sometimes knowing is a matter of getting the right information, the right data. On one occasion at the university we were trying very hard to increase our traditional undergraduate enrollment. We had great people working in our admissions department; an outstanding faculty and staff; strong curriculum offerings that included specialties such as engineering, nursing, and dietetics; and a fine campus. Yet our numbers were flat. We turned to the data.

As we studied the details of our application and enrollment history and practices, a couple of key factors emerged. First, the data revealed that our yield rate (the percentage of students who enroll compared to number of prospects) was slightly above the national average. That single piece of information told us that we were doing a good job recruiting the students in our "pool."

Improving a school's overall yield rate becomes more and more difficult as the rate goes higher. There are so many variables and issues beyond the university's control. The data from our own enrollment history seemed to indicate that although we might be able to increase our yield rate slightly, the real answer lay elsewhere. The implication was simple: to increase the final number of freshmen who enroll, we had to increase the number of total prospects and then improve or at least maintain the same yield rate.

○━━◆━━○

Leadership involves securing, analyzing, and responding to key information.

○━━◆━━○

A second thing revealed by the data was that if we were able to get a student and his or her parents to come to campus for a personal and focused visit, the prospect of that student enrolling was significantly higher. This proved to be a significant piece of information, and based on that insight we assigned a member of the admissions staff to focus only on campus visits. We believed that if we could get the number of campus visits to increase, enrollment would follow. The university also invested in a new admissions center at the campus entrance to make it easier for campus visits to occur.

Leadership involves securing, analyzing, and responding to key information. Without those indicators, the leader is flying without instruments, and although occasionally he or she may see the horizon, often there is only fog.

In addition to getting the right information, another source of knowing comes from talking to the right people. It amazes me how often decisions are made without consulting with key constituents or stakeholders. Do you recall the "new Coke"? When Coca-Cola changed the recipe for Coke several years ago, there was an outcry from coast to coast. People hoarded supplies of the "old Coke" and boycotted the new. The company was bombarded by tens of thousands of calls and letters of protest. Finally, the Coca-Cola Company brought back Coca-Cola "Classic" and pledged to market both the new and the classic Coke. Soon, however, the new Coke simply disappeared. The whole episode might have been avoided if the company would have listened to its own customer base before tampering with the original formula.

Often, knowing goes beyond getting the right information and talking to the right people.

This lesson was reinforced to me not long ago as I participated in the planning for the construction of a major academic building on campus. The key administrators and the architects worked diligently on the plans for the building. We researched the data: how many classrooms, computer labs, and offices were needed. Our plans reflected that input. But it wasn't until we asked several members of the faculty—those who would in fact teach and do other work in that building—for direct input that the plan really came together.

I was so pleased and proud to watch the interchange of ideas and possibilities during those meetings of architects and faculty. I knew that we were going to have a great building because we were getting the information from the right people at the right time in the process.

Often, however, knowing goes beyond getting the right information and talking to the right people. Sometimes knowing requires the leader to simply trust his or her instincts and convictions. As Socrates observed, we begin with the challenge to "know thyself."

A few years ago, I purchased a small sailboat. Since I have the privilege of being a university president, I named my little boat *College Business.* (So if you call and someone tells you that I am out on *college business,* you'll understand.)

When I first hit the water, I was reminded of the three basic rules of boating:

1. Open side up.
2. Pointy end forward.
3. Boats don't go on land.

But beyond this, I learned a few other things as I began to learn to sail. I observed some parallels between sailing and leadership.

1. The importance of the *rudder*

The rudder determines the direction of the boat. In any organization, the rudder is the mission. It is the guiding principle that determines the heading for the organization. Without a steady, confident hand on the rudder, the wind will push the boat to and fro. There may be movement, but the direction will be unclear. The leader's hand certainly guides the organization, but too often a leader assumes that the only hand on the rudder is his or hers. However, in the most effective and efficient organizations, steering is a partnership among all stakeholders because mission must guide everyone's efforts.

2. The importance of the *wind*

You can have a fine boat and a steady hand upon the rudder, but without the wind, there is no power. Many crosscurrents of wind come to bear upon any organization: public opinion; government; demographic, cultural, and financial trends; technology; and politics, to name just a few. Part of any leader's job is to choose the right wind. In so doing, the grace-full leader seeks above all others the winds of the Spirit of God. It is the power and presence of God that must ultimately energize and motivate an organization.

3. The set of the *sail*

On the wall in the lounge of one of our resident halls on campus is a carving and inscription placed there years ago by a professor named Rockwell S. Brank. It is the carving of a sailboat, at full wind, leaning to one side. The inscription says it all: "'Tis not the gale, 'tis the set of the sail, / That determines which way you shall go." The job of a grace-full leader is to man the sails, to catch the winds of the Spirit and be empowered by God for a great task.

4. The *anchor*

Without an anchor, we drift. The anchor holds a ship steady in the storm. Core values and personal faith in God become the anchor to provide stability.

Sailing is a good hobby and a vivid metaphor. About the time I bought my boat, I read a delightful book titled *First You Have to Row a Little Boat*. The writer, Richard Bode, provides a commentary on life by telling about his experiences of learning to sail as a boy. The title comes from his first day on the water. An old sailor agreed to teach him how to sail. The only thing the sailor would let the boy do the first few days was to row a little boat. Bode writes:

> I sat in the center of the dinghy, facing the stern, my destination somewhere behind me, a landfall I couldn't see. I had to judge where I was headed from where I had been, an acquired perception which has served me well—for the goals of my life, and especially my work, haven't always been visible points of light on a shore that looms in front of me. They are fixed in my imagination, shrouded and indistinct, and I detect them best when my eyes are closed. All too often I am forced to move toward them backward, like a

boy in a rowboat, guiding myself by a cultivated inner sense of direction which tells me I am on course, tending toward the place I want to be.

And so in time the rowboat and I became one and the same—like the archer and his bow or the artist and his paint. What I learned wasn't mastery over the elements; it was mastery over myself.[2]

Surely he is right; we must be able to see where we have been in order to chart our course for the future. We must develop an inner sense of direction that keeps us steady in the water. This sense of knowing is vital not only for sailing but also for living and leadership.

The grace-full leader knows he or she must stay in tune with God and follow His leadership.

Einar Kloster, president and CEO of Philips Lighting, observed: "Courage to follow through on your own convictions is critical. You can test your opinions on others, but once you have, you are the one who must decide what to do and whether or not to do it—and it takes courage. Our society is full of Monday morning quarterbacks—people who have all the answers after the fact. You need real courage at those times when you are sitting alone, thinking things through (and deciding what to do next)."[3]

Only when you have the courage of your convictions can you effectively follow your "knows."

Following your "knows" involves getting the right information, talking with the right people, and balancing that input with your instincts and inner compass—but there is more. Ultimately, for the Christian leader, knowing must also include the spiritual dimension. God has promised wisdom and guidance, protection and empowerment. The grace-full leader knows he or she must stay in tune with God and follow His leadership. Of all the things there is to know, knowing God is most important.

Knowing God is more than information; it is relationship. The Old Testament king named Solomon gives a wonderful testimony to the importance of knowing God. Solomon had it all: wisdom, power, and wealth. He possessed everything that people today seem so desperate to attain. Yet, for Solomon, having it all was not enough. It never is enough.

Having looked for peace and contentment in wealth, in work, in pleasure, in nature, and in relationships, Solomon's judgment was that all of this was essentially meaningless. He wrote: "Everything is meaningless. What does man gain from all his labor at which he toils under the sun?" (Eccles. 1:2-3). What a statement. What a question. Such a sense of hopelessness for these opening words of the Book of Ecclesiastes. Solomon, however, is not in despair. He is simply declaring what is ultimately true: if a person does not know God, everything else is meaningless. And he returns to that message in a very revealing way at the end of the book: "Now all has been heard; here is the conclusion of the matter: Fear God and keep his commandments, for this is the whole duty of man" (12:13). The grace-full leader understands that the first "know" to follow is knowing God.

If you are to step out into the unknown, the place to begin is with the exploration of the inner territory.
—James Kouzes and Barry Posner

Then Jesus said to his disciples, "If anyone would come after me, he must deny himself and take up his cross and follow me."
—Matt. 16:24

14

GRACE-*full* LEADERS . . .

are willing to follow as well as lead

An oxymoron is a combination of contradictory or incongruous words and concepts. For example: bittersweet, giant shrimp, student teacher, civil war, second best, death benefits, old news, sweet sorrow, thunderous silence, life insurance, genuine imitation, and my personal favorite—rap music!

The list could go on, for there seems to be no end to oxymorons in contemporary life. I suppose that "a leader who follows" might, at first glance, appear to be an oxymoron as well. However, the grace-full leader knows that learning to follow is one of the first great lessons of leadership.

This idea of leaders as followers may take some getting used to for some. It seems just the opposite of the normal role of leadership, which is commonly understood as being out front, pointing the way, and giving the orders.

Several years ago, a fellow named Hugh VanVoorst announced his retirement from United Airlines. Hugh is a friend of mine and a businessman in the community where I live, but his primary profession was a commercial airline pilot. He flew jumbo jets from Chicago to Europe several times a month.

Rather than the traditional retirement party, Hugh decided to take his family and a few friends on a bit of a joyride in a Boeing 757. So he leased one of those planes for an evening. Jill and I were invited, but for some reason (I think it was the thunder and lightning that evening), Jill decided not to go. But I thought it would be great fun.

∘━◆━∘

Before long we were on the runway
with those great jet engines hurling us
forward into the early evening sky.

∘━◆━∘

I drove to O'Hare Airport in Chicago, parked my car, entered the terminal, and consulted the big board of departures and arrivals. And there, sure enough, nestled in among all of the listings of the various airline flights, was a single line: "Hugh Van-Voorst Retirement Flight—Gate B-7."

I walked through the security checkpoint and down the concourse to gate B-7, where the party was already under way. There were balloons, streamers, cards, coffee, and cake. Hugh was there, along with his family and several friends from the area. Hugh introduced us all to the cabin crew and a gentleman who would be his copilot for the flight. Soon we were handed boarding passes, and we walked through the Jetway onto this flight of fancy.

Hugh told us that we would be back in Chicago in a couple of hours, but he had never told us where we were headed. Nonetheless, we settled into our seats, watched as the safety video was played, and felt the plane back slowly away from the terminal.

Before long we were on the runway with those great jet engines hurling us forward into the early evening sky. Soon we were soaring. The lights of the great city of Chicago were spread out before us like diamonds on a jeweler's black velvet cloth. In the distance the lightning flashed as that great plane turned to the west.

In the cabin, people got up and walked around, visited, helped themselves to snacks, and swapped stories about how we had all come to know Hugh VanVoorst. After we had been aloft for a while, Hugh came on the intercom and told us that we were now over Iowa and would soon turn back to the east. He said that when we got near our destination, he would come back on.

Conversation died down after a while, and most of us were seated when Hugh made his announcement concerning our destination. He said that we were now headed for the little airport in our hometown of Kankakee, Illinois, and would arrive there within the next few minutes. A nervous laugh rippled through the cabin. You see, most of us had been to the Kankakee Airport. It's a nice little airport, right by the interstate, just south of town. But none of us could imagine how Hugh was going to land a Boeing 757 on that little airstrip. And added to that wee bit of anxiety, the lightning, which had been off in the distance, was now quite close. The windows were being pelted with rain.

But sure enough, as we came down through the clouds, there was Kankakee. The flickering lights of Kennedy Drive and

Court Street were visible, and just beyond the interstate, the airport. The plane banked, and we buckled up tightly.

The plane got lower and lower, and the city drew closer as the jet appeared to be settling in for a landing. Just before we reached the airport, we crossed Interstate 57. Cars began to pull off onto the side of the road. Then, being very low, we roared just above the parking lot of a local restaurant. People with take-home buckets of chicken ran for cover, pointing in disbelief.

As we held our breath, Hugh came back on the intercom and put us at ease by telling us that we would not actually be landing at the airport. He had made arrangements with the FAA for us to make "an approach"—that is, to come in as if we were going to land, but then, just before touching down, to pull it up and be on our way. So, just above the airport runway, we felt the thrust of the engines as the giant jet turned once more for the sky. Everyone cheered and clapped and laughed.

From Kankakee, we made a big loop over into Indiana and then headed back to Chicago. About 20 minutes before touchdown, a flight attendant came to me and said I was invited to the cockpit. So I made my way forward and entered what seemed to me to be a very small cabin. Hugh said, "Hey, Doc, I thought you might want to see this."

The storm, which had been coming toward us ever so slowly, was now settled in like heavy syrup over Chicago. It wasn't violent, but it did coat the city with a dense wet night fog. The brilliant spangle of lights we had seen at takeoff was now invisible.

Just behind Hugh was a little jump seat that folded down from the wall. He said, "Sit down and strap yourself in." Without hesitation, I did just as I was told. And what I saw and heard during the next few moments I will never forget.

In addition to all of the dials and gauges and gadgets in a cockpit, there was, just in front of the pilot, a computer screen with a bright-colored background, a line (which appeared to me to be the horizon), some accompanying mathematical coordinates, and the image of a plane.

"Did you know that these planes can land themselves?" Hugh turned to me and asked.

"I didn't know that," I replied with a slight quiver in my voice.

"We do it all the time," he said. "It's simply a matter of having the right set of coordinates. Once you are locked on the beam, it will bring you safely in."

And sure enough, as I sat there in the darkness, Hugh began a conversation with the tower. He told this invisible voice where he was, where he had been, and where he was headed. In reply, through the darkness and storm, came a calm voice of comfort. "I've got you," he said. "Change your course to such and such."

He said, "It's simply a matter of having the right set of coordinates. Once you're locked on the beam, it will bring you safely in."

Hugh entered those coordinates into the computer, and that great flying ship began to turn and descend. In just a moment we heard, "You're on beam," from the tower. From that moment on, little by little, we descended in a slow, steady slope toward an invisible O'Hare Field. The runway was not visible when Hugh told the passengers in the cabin to prepare for landing. Then suddenly, as if someone had rolled back a great black blanket, we broke through the clouds to see the lights of the runway and . . . we were down.

What a night—what a flight! I remember it all quite clearly, but the single memory that stuck with me more than any other was Hugh's comment about landing that plane in poor visibility. He said, "It's simply a matter of having the right set of coordinates. Once you're locked on the beam, it will bring you safely in."

That is true for all of life, isn't it? It is certainly true for those who lead others. We can lead only as we follow.

On the day I was inaugurated as president of Olivet Nazarene University, I entered the convocation center as the last person in the academic processional; and then, at the end of the ceremony, the order was reversed, and I led the way out. The symbolism was significant. I wanted to demonstrate that I was first a follower, one who walked in the footsteps of all who had gone before me, a long line of individuals who forged and fostered the corporate life of the school. And then I was a leader.

In my brief response during the ceremony, I told a story I heard from Willis Lambert. I had the privilege of serving as Willis's pastor for several years. At the time he was a funeral director. We had a variety of interesting experiences together. On one occasion we came out of the church following a funeral service to prepare for the trip to the cemetery, only to find that the funeral cars had been stolen. We made a few quick calls, borrowed a couple of replacement vehicles from a neighboring mortuary, and continued our duties.

As we traveled to the cemetery, I asked Willis if he had ever experienced anything like that before. He said, "No, not exactly," but then went on to tell me about a funeral service a few weeks prior. When it came time for the trip to the cemetery, rather than riding with the funeral director, the officiating pastor made arrangements for his personal car to be positioned just after the lead car in the line of cars for the processional. The pastor's house was near the cemetery, and he thought it would be more convenient to have his own car at the graveside.

Everything went smoothly as the long line of cars made its way across the city toward the cemetery. Evidently, however, the pastor's mind began to wander; and rather than continuing to follow the lead car toward the cemetery, when the procession reached the street where he normally turned to go home, the pastor made his usual turn. It was not until he pulled into his driveway that he realized that the entire procession had continued to follow him.

Grace-full leaders know the importance of following.

Balance isn't either/or; it's and.
—Stephen R. Covey

In all your ways acknowledge him, and he will make your paths straight.
—Prov. 3:6

15

GRACE-*full* LEADERS . . .
maintain their balance

Balance is one of the great principles of leadership and of life itself. This is particularly true in an age of excess and in a culture that fosters a "me first" mind-set. The grace-full leader must learn to manage competing priorities; to maintain the long view in the midst of daily demands; and to balance work and leisure, church and family, tasks and people.

By its very definition, balance suggests competing forces and values. Balance gives a leader the ability to walk the tightrope of opposing priorities without falling off. Balance is crucial in at least two important areas: balancing the demands of leadership itself and balancing work with the rest of life.

Balancing the Demands of Leadership

Leadership is a three-legged stool—a combination of competence, character, and will. Each leg must be in place if the stool is to stand. If a person does not have at least some measure of all three, he or she cannot lead. But having these characteristics alone is not enough—they must be balanced.

Imagine someone whose will to lead far exceeds his or her competence or character. That has the making of a demagogue. Likewise, if a person has high competency but little will to lead or character fit for leadership, he or she becomes a technocrat—a person who knows but can't translate that knowledge into effective leadership. One with appropriate character but little or no competency or will to lead also falls short of all that it is required for effective leadership. Some individuals can survive for a time with two of the three legs in place, but when times of testing come, their leadership falls short. The effective leader maintains the delicate balance of all three components.

An effective leader must learn to establish and maintain the proper balance between leading and managing. A leader can very quickly forfeit his or her leadership potential and effectiveness by becoming too preoccupied with managing the organization. Both are necessary, but the leader must always lead first, manage when and where it's necessary, and learn to delegate the bulk of the work of management.

Leaders are interested in vision, goals, direction, objectives, purpose, and effectiveness. Managers, on the other hand, are primarily concerned with efficiency, the how-to, and the day to day of getting the work done. Management is about today, and leadership is about tomorrow. Leaders do the right things, while managers do things right. A good organization must have both. Warren Bennis has developed a list of helpful distinctions between managers and leaders:

- The manager administers; the leader innovates.
- The manager is a copy; the leader is an original.
- The manager maintains; the leader develops.

- The manager focuses on systems and structures; the leader focuses on people.
- The manager relies on control; the leader inspires trust.
- The manager has a short-term view; the leader has a long-term view.
- The manager asks when and how; the leader asks what and why.
- The manager has her eye on the bottom line; the leader has her eye on the horizon.[1]

Often organizations falter because they are overmanaged and underled. Balance is the key.

There must also be a sense of balance among the various demands and constituents of a job. Because I have spent much of my working life in a university setting, I was particularly intrigued with an observation made by Clark Kerr in his classic volume titled *The Uses of the University*. This provides a bit of commentary on the role of a college president:

> The university president in the United States is expected to be a friend of the students, a colleague of the faculty, a good fellow with the alumni, a sound administrator with the trustees, a good speaker with the public, an astute bargainer with the foundations and the federal agencies, a politician with the state legislature, a friend of industry, labor, and agriculture, a persuasive diplomat with donors, a champion of education generally, a supporter of the professions, a spokesman to the press, a scholar in his own right, a public servant, a devotee of opera and football equally, a decent human being, a good husband and father, an active member of a church. Above all, he must enjoy traveling in airplanes, eating his meals in public, and attending public ceremonies.
>
> He should be firm, yet gentle; sensitive to others, insensitive to himself; look to the past and the future, yet be

firmly planted in the present; both visionary and sound; affable, yet reflective; know the value of a dollar and realize that ideas cannot be bought; inspiring in his visions, yet cautious in what he does; a man of principle, yet able to make a deal. No one can be all of these things. Some succeed at being none.[2]

A proper balance will ensure that an individual meets at least most of the expectations associated with his or her work. But balance must also extend beyond the work environment.

Balancing Between Work and Life

A leader needs to have balance at work as well as recognize the sensitive balance between work and the rest of life, including family, community service, and leisure. The place to begin is taking and keeping control of your schedule. Only then can time be given to the most important things in life. You cannot keep balance for long if control is relinquished to someone else.

In controlling your time, a leader need not become enslaved to work or to the ideas, schedules, and designs of other people. It's important to schedule prime time for yourself. That is not selfish or insensitive; it is balance. Notice in the Gospels how often Jesus withdrew from the crowd and even from His closest disciples so that He might be alone. If He needed that, how much more do we.

Steven Covey records this testimony from a busy executive.

In the last seventeen years of being a business executive, I've taken a lot of people out to lunch. But as I wrote out my roles and came to "husband," I realized that I hadn't been taking my own wife out for lunch. And my relationship with her is one of the most important relationships in my life.

So, as a result of weekly organizing, we started doing that, and it's brought us much closer. Our communication has increased, which has led me to discover other ways I can be a better husband. As I review my role as a husband each week I believe I'm doing a much better job.[3]

Leaders who go the distance have learned that they are better at work if they consistently take time away from the demands of leadership to bring balance and perspective to their lives. Balanced individuals are socially active, keep up on current events, maintain a healthy sense of humor, and are active physically. They read, watch, observe, and learn.

⊙━━◆━━○

Grace-full leaders maintain balance
by choosing carefully among all
of the options available.

⊙━━◆━━○

Balance in life prevents becoming an extremist or being eccentric in beliefs, attitudes, and actions. It keeps the pressures of success and failure in proper balance. Dealing with adversity and prosperity are both two extreme tests. Both challenge your ability to remain steady and focused and to keep spiritual equilibrium. And of the two, perhaps success is the hardest. The Scottish essayist and historian Thomas Carlyle observed: "Adversity is hard on a man, but for one man who can stand prosperity, there are a hundred that will stand adversity."[4]

Grace-full leaders maintain balance by choosing carefully among all of the options available. They travel light.

Let's visit the International Terminal at O'Hare Airport in Chicago. Several flights are preparing to leave for the four corners of the globe, and just as many are landing. Our ears perk to the sounds of many languages. Our eyes race from face to face as we see the people of the world passing before us as a colorful human palette.

At the Air France ticket counter 30 young college students are preparing for the adventure of a lifetime. They are going to study in France for one year. The initial instructions indicated that each student might check a maximum of 44 pounds of luggage, plus carry-on luggage. The first young lady steps forward and heaves her suitcase on the scales: 42 pounds. Then the young man behind the Air France desk says to her, "Your other bag please."

"Oh, this isn't to be weighed; I'm going to carry it on," she replies.

"Oh, but it is!" he answers.

Reluctantly she places her other piece of luggage on the scales. "Twenty-three pounds," says the young man. "That means you are 21 pounds over the weight limit. You may try to eliminate some of your luggage or pay an extra charge of $105."

The word spreads through the line of young people like a grass fire. Suddenly there is no line. The students scatter, luggage begins to open like popcorn; everyone is suddenly trying to lighten his or her load. It's sheer bedlam: items are being tossed with abandon—extra dresses, jackets, shoes, soap, an iron, a five-pound fruitcake in the shape of Illinois, books, batteries, baseball gloves. It looks like a giant garage sale.

Each student is deciding what is "essential" for the journey; each is determining what he or she can live without. It's a challenging assignment, but they make it and soon depart on schedule, leaving their parents to carry so much stuff back to the cars that the customs officers want to know from where this group has just arrived.

This imaginary airport experience is a metaphor of life and leadership. Over time, most of us accumulate some excess baggage—things we unnecessarily hang on to, things we deposit in our memory banks and pack into our emotional suitcases to carry with us from place to place. Many folks go through life carrying suitcases filled with memories, gathered up, one by one, in moments of rejection or regret. The result, over time, is that we drag ourselves from day to day, weighted down by the past.

It's hard to be joyful when you carry a burden. It's hard to love when you are weighted down. Too often, in fact, we find ourselves throwing stones as well as carrying them. Each year the baggage gets heavier, so much so that after a while, we either break down under the load or pay dearly for it in some other way, or we find a way to lighten our loads.

Leaders know that they must continually lighten their loads if they are going to continue to lead. Part of learning to balance is to reduce the load and equalize the remaining pressures. Jesus has a good word for us. The good news of the gospel is that we can lay aside our burdens and learn to travel light. Jesus said: "Come to me, all you who are weary and burdened, and I will give you rest. Take my yoke upon you and learn from me, for I am gentle and humble in heart, and you will find rest for your souls. For my yoke is easy and my burden is light" (Matt. 11:28-30).

These are words not just for the weary person in general, but for the weary leader in particular. As you read through the Gospels, one thing becomes clear: Jesus spent quite a bit of time getting rid of excess baggage. On one occasion He spoke of the Pharisees as those who "tie up heavy loads and put them on men's shoulders" (Matt. 23:4).

Jesus traveled light. When He was asked about keeping the law, He replied that the entire law is fulfilled by loving the Lord your God with all your heart and loving your neighbor as yourself. The call of Christ is not to a complicated system of religious rituals, rules, and regulations. Rather, His focus is on relationships. If the relationship is genuine, the other issues follow in a natural way. Life pushes us down and out; Jesus draws us in and up.

If you are carrying some excess baggage on the journey, Jesus says, "Come to Me, check your bags here, and I will give you rest."

If you don't have a dream, how can you have a dream come true?
—Faye LaPointe

Where there is no vision, the people perish.
—Prov. 29:1

16

GRACE-*full* LEADERS . . .
have double vision

Vision grabs. Initially it grabs the leader, then those who follow. To be an effective leader, you need vision—an idea greater than the present. But you must also be able to communicate that vision to others in ways that emotionally, mentally, and volitionally enable them to turn this vision into reality. Vision means little if it's not translated into action.

Theodore Hesburgh, the distinguished former president of the University of Notre Dame, says that vision is the very essence of leadership. "Know where you want to go. That requires three things: having a clear vision, articulating it well, and getting your team enthusiastic about sharing it. Above all, any leader must be consistent. As the Bible says, no one follows an uncertain trumpet."[1]

Without vision, leadership is little more than simple perpetuation of the past instead of predication on the future. A proper vision builds on the past by allowing room for new ideas and thoughts. Leaders hold in their minds pictures and ideals of what can be. They are positive about the future and ardently believe that working together, people can make a difference.

Imagine someone deciding to build a huge factory: buying the land, hiring an architect and builder, arranging the financing, bringing the project to completion, assembling all the machinery, hiring a workforce, and then sitting down to ask: "What product should we manufacture? What's supposed to go out those double doors of the shipping department and on to semitrailers and railroad cars? Why did we build this factory?"

No one starts a work and moves then to mission. Leadership starts with a mission and a vision that, in turn, shapes the work and uses the resources available to accomplish the mission. Vision drives—not follows—a great work.

A problem, however, sometimes develops as people join a work in progress and begin to function as part of the organization without ever really owning the dream or possessing the vision that gave birth and continues to sustain the work being done. If you were hired in the midst of building the factory, for example, that might be all you would do at first. It could be easy under those circumstances to become convinced that the work of that particular business is the building and the maintenance of the factory itself. It is dangerously easy for a means to become an end in itself.

*Most often you get that for which you
have planned and worked.*

Apart from a few entrepreneurs, most people have joined a work already in progress. And often we are called upon to spend so much of our time and energy building and managing the organization that those endeavors become ends in themselves, and we fail to ask the important questions: "What is the vision? Why are we doing this? What is the reason for all of the effort and toil? What is our mission? Where will we be when we get where we're going?"

Grace-full leaders recognize that good things rarely just happen. Most often you get that for which you have planned and worked. A college degree, for example, doesn't simply arrive in the mail unsolicited. You plan for it, envision it, apply for it, work for it, and pay a significant price in dollars, sweat, and tears. But that very difficult process bestows value. So success comes when the last assignment is done and the last exam taken and the last period on the last page of the last paper is finally printed, when the line is formed and your name is called, the degree is handed to you in the midst of great ceremony, and you move in that moment from being an undergraduate to a graduate—you experience the satisfying thrill of achievement. You paid the price, over time, and gained, therefore, something of great value.

No organization, no church, or no institution within the church can function effectively when it loses sight of its mission; for most of the time in life, you get what you expect. Tell me your vision, and I will tell you your future.

For the grace-full leader, vision and faith are inseparably linked, for "faith is . . . the evidence of things not seen" (Heb. 11:1, KJV). Faith is vision, and vision is seeing it long before it is. Growing and vibrant organizations expect and plan, in advance, to grow. Much of life is a self-fulfilling prophecy.

Leadership demands that you see both what is and what can be. This "double vision" helps enable us to keep our sights set on the future as we deal with the daily demands of leadership.

Double vision also helps one see the potential that people have. One of the most distinguished sculptors in American history was a man named Gutzon Borglum. He was a sculptor on a grand scale who is perhaps best known for his bust of Abraham Lincoln at the U.S. Capitol in Washington, D.C. On that project he carved the head of Lincoln from a large block of marble that had long been in his studio.

The woman who cleaned his work area had swept around the formless mass of marble day after day for a long time. Then one day, as Borglum's work progressed, she began to see the face of Lincoln emerging from the stone. She quickly turned and, looking at Borglum, asked, "Is that master Lincoln?"

"Yes," he replied.

"How did you know he was in there?" she asked.

The great sculptor knew, for he had double vision. All great artists have such a gift. They see what is and what can be. Every leader needs that same characteristic. That vision is a gift of grace.

○═╾═○

The leader transforms
mission into vision.

○═╾═○

God could see a great king in the shepherd boy named David. He saw Peter, the Rock, in an impulsive fisherman named Simon. He could see the apostle Paul in one named Saul of Tarsus. God has placed great potential in every human life, and the wise and grace-full leader can be used of God to enable people to reach their full potential.

Experts in business management remind us that a clearly defined mission is essential to every organization. The leader transforms mission into vision. He or she defines what mission looks like. To lead is to cast a vision. All businesses, organizations, projects, and products begin in the mind's eye. Leaders begin with imagination and the belief that what is merely an image can one day be made real.[2]

"To choose a direction, a leader must first have developed a mental image of a possible and desirable future state of the organization. This image, which we call a vision, may be as vague as a dream or as precise as a goal or mission statement. The critical point is that a vision articulates a view of a realistic, credible, attractive future for the organization, a condition that is better in some important ways than what now exists."[3]

Grace-full leaders are not just managers, but visionary leaders. They provide the leadership necessary for any given group or organization to fully realize its mission and potential. This level of leadership goes beyond the daily problem solving associated with management to the exploiting of opportunities. Simply solving problems only restores the status quo. It does not necessarily advance the organization.

Effective, grace-full leadership actively links vision and faith, for they are essentially one. Vision is vital to faith. Scripture teaches, "Now faith is being sure of what we hope for and certain of what we do not see" (Heb. 11:1). What a wonderful description of vision this is.

When Abraham, one of the greatest examples of faith and leadership in the entire Bible, was called by God to leave his homeland, he was given a great vision of what God was going to bring to pass through him. The vision was a central part of what Abraham needed for his journey. And with faith, invigorated by this vision, Abraham was empowered not only to make this great pilgrimage but also to lead others in this journey. Vision suggests a future. A proper vision sets the orientation of the entire organization on to new possibilities.

○━╋━○

People hunger to give their time and
energies to something larger
than themselves.

○━╋━○

A vivid image from my boyhood is Dr. Martin Luther King Jr. standing on the steps of the Lincoln Memorial addressing a crowd of 250,000 people. As he spoke, he cast a vision. He spoke of the possibility of a new and better future, not just for Black Americans, but for all Americans. He proclaimed, "I have a dream." He was articulate, enthusiastic, optimistic, and uplifting. His dream and his vision moved the nation.

People hunger to give their time and energies to something larger than themselves. Leaders who offer that will have no shortage of followers. People will consistently work harder and longer when they understand the overall significance of how their work fits with the total mission.

Visions are statements of destination, and destination determines the direction and objectives of an organization. I live one hour directly south of the city of Chicago. When I leave my house to travel into the city, all of my actions must be conditioned by that destination if my vision of a trip to Chicago is to be realized. To get to Chicago, I must head north. If I turn my car to the east, away from that destination, all of my actions from that moment on, no matter how good or well intentioned, will not contribute to the accomplishment of my vision of a trip to the city. Everything else—my speed, the kind of vehicle I drive, the traffic, the scenery along the road—loses its meaning if the destination is not clearly defined and constantly in focus.

Vision also carries with it a sense of the possible. The balance between casting a vision that is indeed attainable and one viewed as impossible is a fine line. If a vision is perceived as so grand that it cannot be realized, it can serve to defeat an organization rather than inspire. Yet, if a leader casts a vision that has no challenge, it will likewise fail to motivate.

Visions are conceptualizations. Just as architects and engineers make drawings and models, leaders cast visions to create an image of what can be. The primary public television station in our area is WTTW from Chicago. Using those letters as an acronym, the station has developed the slogan "WTTW—Your Window To The World." I think of vision in much the same way. Vision is your window to the world of the future. What you learn to see as a leader ultimately shapes your vision.

○══╋══○

Grace transforms our vision
and brings spiritual focus.

○══╋══○

My father spent a lifetime in the newspaper business. When we went on family vacations, each day, wherever we were, my dad bought a local newspaper. He would look through the paper, noting all the technical features: the weight of the newsprint, the style of type, the layout, the number of column inches given to advertising, and so on. He could often tell the type of press that was used just by looking the paper over carefully.

Now my mom, when she picked up this same paper, read the human interest stories and looked through the ads. My older brother read the sports page and the comics. And me, I pretty much looked out the window—reading someone else's hometown newspaper wasn't my idea of a vacation. The point is this: you see what you have eyes to see. We all had eyes and all had access to the same thing, but each of us saw and experienced it differently. Vision is a "see" word. It evokes images and pictures.

Think of watching a slide show. What if each picture was out of focus? Not only would you quickly lose interest, but also you'd experience frustration or confusion. In one sense a leader controls the projector. The most important role of visions in organizational life is to give focus to human energy. Visions are like lenses. They enable everyone to see more clearly what lies ahead.

Grace transforms our vision and brings spiritual focus. Jesus consistently conveyed to His followers the importance of their work, and He offered ordinary people the opportunity to be part of something extraordinary. His call to men mending their nets was, "Come, follow me . . . and I will make you fishers of men" (Matt. 4:19). It was a larger, more significant vision. Graceful leaders see both what is and what might be!

Go as far as you can see; when you get there, you'll be able to see farther.
—Thomas Carlyle

When [Jesus] had finished speaking, he said to Simon,
"Put out into deep water."
—Luke 5:4

17

GRACE-*full* LEADERS . . .
"go deep"

Leadership is a little like surfing. If you want to surf, you have to get out to where the big waves are. You can't ride the board on waves that are ankle deep. You can't spend your time paddling around in the little pools near the shore. You've got to get out where the white water runs. Going deep is the first thing you have to do if you are going to catch the big wave.

If you paddle a surfboard out to where the water is well over your head, you begin to feel the rhythm of the sea. You feel the waves building and wait for the right one. As it rises, you ride just in front of it, at first, and let it lift you. Then, just as it begins to crest, you stand in one smooth motion, just as though you are standing up on land, and plant your feet firmly on the board. Then you lean back just a little and move the board to the crest where the power is, and suddenly you are riding the wave. The whole ocean roars around you. It sounds like ten thousand yards of tearing silk. That tremendous yowl surges up under you. The surfboard trembles at your feet. It's a magnificent experience to be riding the curl of the wave. There is power and speed and exhilaration. It is unbelievable.

There is a leadership experience much like that for those who will "go deep." If you are going to lead, you can't hug the shore and splash around in shallow water.

You see, shallow water
- breeds shallow people
- presents no challenge and therefore yields no reward
- fosters caution rather than courage
- produces superficial thinking
- yields immature behavior
- results in only surface relationships

But deep water brings an abundant catch and produces men and women of depth and character, men and women fit for life. Jesus said, "I have come that they may have life, and have it to the full" (John 10:10). Abundant living—that's what God wants for you.

Shallow water people never know abundance. They never know that we serve a great and glorious God, One whose very presence can lift us and propel us forward in exhilarating new ways. Grace-full leaders are white-water people, living out where the breakers roll and the surge of the sea unleashes its power and its bounty.

Once in a while when you are surfing, an exceptional wave comes along; and if your timing is good, you can crest the curl, come down the other side, and turn into the wave so that the wave itself curls over your head. In that moment, you find yourself in a tunnel of thundering water. It swirls all about you like a whirling, watery cathedral.

The sheet of water above you is so thin that the sunlight coming down through it spangles as if a shower of gems is cascading about you. And strangely enough, it is very quiet in there, and it's peaceful, and you can lean back a little against the wall of water behind you as it lifts you and carries you along.

But you will never have this experience, you will never know what it's like to be swept along in the midst of a crystal cathedral until you move out into the midst of the wave—until you say yes to all that God calls you to be and all He has for you to do.

Grace-full leaders . . . are men and women who are willing to get their feet wet.

At the end of the day you drag yourself and your surfboard up onto the beach and ram the board into the sand. You fall down in front of it, lean back against it, and listen as the roar of the sea subsides, as if to acknowledge the fact that you have won.

In the distance, the setting sun cuts itself on the tops of the waves and bleeds across the water right to your feet. You are exhausted, your teeth are loose, and you ache all over—but oh, what a thrill. The ride, the risk, the tumbles and spills, the ups and downs have all been worth it, for you have pushed out into the deep and ridden with the waves.

Grace-full leaders go deep. They are men and women who are willing to get their feet wet. Have you ever thought about how many idioms relate to your feet? We talk about putting our best foot forward, gaining a foothold, getting your feet wet, getting off on the right foot. We speak of being footloose or having two left feet. We drag our feet, toe the line, and even put our foot down from time to time. And of course, there are times when we put our foot in our mouth. Having cold feet indicates fear of commitment and the unknown. It's more commonly used for backing out of a marriage, but it also happens to people in leadership because leadership involves risk. And risk often travels with its first cousin, fear.

There are times in the life of any leader when he or she will have to make a decision between having cold feet or wet feet. When those moments come, grace-full leaders go deep. For example, consider an experience described in the opening section of Joshua. The Old Testament portion of the Bible is, for the most part, the story of one great family—a family that became a nation and the biblical "people of God." The Old Testament is the story of Abraham and his descendants, known to us today as the Jewish people. The Old Testament calls these folks the children of Israel.

As we join their story in the Book of Joshua, the leader of the Israelites, Moses, has died, and the leadership of the people has fallen to a man named Joshua. It is now Joshua's task to lead the children of Israel in the next phase of their journey, which happens to be the conquest of the Promised Land.

God had long ago promised Abraham a homeland for his descendants. That promise was renewed generation after generation; and now, finally, after hundreds of years, the descendants of Abraham are ready to take the land, with Joshua leading them into the reality of this promise.

Isn't it interesting that although God had promised His people this land and brought them to its threshold, it was up to them, with His help, to conquer and possess it? The right leader had to be in place for this to happen.

More than 3,000 years ago the people of God prepared to cross the Jordan River into the Promised Land. Joshua 3:5 is one great sentence: "Joshua told the people, 'Consecrate yourselves,

for tomorrow the LORD will do amazing things among you.'"
Joshua was convinced that God wanted to do "amazing things"
for His people, and I remind you that God has not changed. He
is still a God who keeps His promises and longs to do "amazing
things" among His people.

Joshua, following the Lord's instructions, gets everything
ready; and in verses 14-16 we read, "So when the people broke
camp to cross the Jordan, the priests carrying the ark of the covenant went ahead of them. Now the Jordan is at flood stage all
during harvest. Yet as soon as the priests who carried the ark
reached the Jordan and their feet touched the water's edge, the
water from upstream stopped flowing."

Then at verse 17, "The priests who carried the ark of the
covenant of the LORD stood firm on dry ground in the middle of
the Jordan, while all Israel passed by until the whole nation had
completed the crossing on dry ground."

Here is the story of a group of people who have come to a
moment of promise but also to a moment of apparent impossibility. Before them is the Jordan River at flood stage. There are
no bridges, no ferries, no pontoons, yet the instructions from the
Lord are for the priests to lead the people into the water. Can't
you just hear the priests who were at the front of that line?

"After you."

"No, you go first."

"Oh, no, no, you go ahead; I have a stone in my sandal—I'll
catch up with you."

It would have been a frightening moment for these people,
in Joshua's day, to march right into a raging river at flood stage.
Most of what they wanted in life—the promise of their future—
lay just before them on the other side of this obstacle. But they
had a choice to make: do they get cold feet and turn away, or
will they trust God enough to get their feet wet?

○━━✦━━○

I have observed that things happen
when God's people are willing to take
the risk of getting their feet wet.

○━━✦━━○

I have observed that things happen when God's people are willing to take the risk of getting their feet wet. And, sure enough, there must have been an audible gasp as those first priests put their feet into the waters of the flood-swollen Jordan River. And then the nation watched with faith and astonishment as the Lord intervened and the river parted and the people of God walked across on dry ground.

Grace-full leaders know that having wet feet rather than cold feet means they must start—must be willing to take those first steps of leadership. No matter how unlikely the timing or difficult the circumstances or impossible the task, it falls to the leader to lead.

Joshua, who by now was 80 years old, might have very well questioned the timing of this call to cross the river. Why not years before when he was younger? Or why not even days before when the river was not at flood tide?

Here they are ready

+ to cross over to their inheritance,
+ to move on to better days,
+ to come face-to-face with their future—

but just before them is an obstacle.

How true to life that is. Most good things in life lie just beyond some obstacle or some challenge. Times of great challenge are often the times when the greatness of God is revealed. Leaders must be people whose faith is sufficient to step out and begin the journey to the future.

The timing appeared to be bad and the circumstances difficult, but under Joshua's leadership these people were willing to start. They got their feet wet. They gave God a chance to be God.

○━━◆━━○

Many of us simply don't make enough
room in our lives for God to be God.

○━━◆━━○

Many of us simply don't make enough room in our lives for God to be God. We only go as far as we can see—we don't leave room for God to do something great in our lives. I think there is a challenge for any leader in this story. What are you going to do when the water gets deep and the going gets tough? Are you going to get cold feet, or trust God and just keep going? The life of every leader is filled with moments when he or she must trust.

I was in Chicago a couple of years ago on a beautiful sunny day. I had walked from Water Tower to State Street, and on my way back I walked up Michigan Avenue. Just as I reached the Chicago River, bells began to sound and lights began to flash, and a huge set of gates crossed before me, closing the sidewalk and street.

As soon as the way was cleared, someone seated in the tower at river's edge must have pulled what was to me an invisible lever; and suddenly, dramatically, the street before me parted, and that great bridge on Michigan Avenue rose in two sections toward the sky. All the traffic—pedestrians, cars, trucks, bicycles, taxicabs, horse-drawn buggies, limousines—came to a stop, for here, in the very heart of the city, this drawbridge had opened.

I excitedly thought that some big ship was about to pass directly in front of me on the Chicago River. I looked west up the river, but I couldn't see it. I looked east toward the lake, but I saw no ship. I then looked down, and passing by in the water was a little private sailboat, with a pretty tall mast—probably just tall enough to reach the bridge.

The captain of that little ship had, evidently, radioed the controller seated high above, and what had seemed like an impossibility suddenly happened as the bridge itself split in two and stood at attention for this little boat.

Later that day, a cabdriver told me that any boat on the river has the right-of-way. When a boat comes through, whether at midnight or noon, the traffic stops and the bridge opens.

Grace-full leaders have not only starting power but also staying power.

I am convinced that grace-full leaders have a similar right-of-way. As a leader, you may come up against some great obstacle, at the most inopportune time; but if you will let it be known to the One who sits forever at the controls of this world, then like the people of Joshua's day, your difficulty will divide before you, and you will cross over. You must be willing to risk wet feet to find faith's solid ground.

Having wet feet rather than cold feet means you must be willing to start, but it also means you must be willing to stand. It is one thing to start. It is another thing, having started, to be willing to stand, to hold steady, to stay the course, to be true, to remain faithful.

Some people get cold feet partway along the journey. They start with great enthusiasm, but when the going gets tough, their feet get tender. Grace-full leaders have not only starting power but also staying power.

If it had not been for the wind in my face,
I wouldn't have been able to fly at all.
—Arthur Ashe

Each man will be like a shelter from the wind and a refuge from the storm, like
streams of water in the desert and the shadow of a great rock in a thirsty land.
—Isa. 32:2

18
GRACE-*full* LEADERS . . .
are skilled meteorologists

Human beings live *on* the solid portion of the earth's surface but *in,* and at the bottom *of,* a sea of air that is many times deeper than any ocean. This sea of air is commonly called the atmosphere, and it has certain characteristics that greatly influence human life. Of the various elements surrounding us in the natural environment, climate and weather are among the most important.

Weather is the sum total of atmospheric conditions for a short period of time; climate is the general or overall total of those conditions over a long period of time. Climate and weather affect what lives and grows in a certain area. The vegetation of the rain forest is different from the vegetation at the top of Pikes Peak.

Every organization has a "climate." A skilled leader knows how to react to various organizational weather patterns—storms, calm, high pressure, thunder, and lightning. Leadership is, in many ways, a foul-weather job because that's when a leader is

155

most severely tested. One cannot always avoid the winds, the snow, and the sleet, but a leader can prepare for them. Anticipating the storm is one key responsibility of a leader.

An effective leader is both weather forecaster and weather factor. By this I mean that a leader functions both as a person who watches and understands the changing patterns of corporate and organization weather and as one who creates certain weather patterns. It is the difference between a thermometer and a thermostat. A thermometer only registers the temperature; a thermostat controls it. Effective leaders do both.

Understanding the Weather That Affects Organizations

It was a cold, clear, moonless night. The stars twinkled across the night sky. Their reflected light danced like fireflies on the calm, dark waters of the North Atlantic.

Inside the Grand Salon, crystal chandeliers bathed passengers in a golden glow as the band played on into the night. In the First Class Club Room, millionaires gathered for cigars, cards, and cognac. On the second- and third-class decks many were already asleep as the greatest ship on earth cut its record-breaking path through the sea.

It was late, almost midnight, when one lone lookout saw the dark ice in the distance. Had there been a full moon, perhaps he could have spotted the danger sooner. If only there had been some wind, foam from the waves breaking against the massive mountains of moving ice might have been visible in the starlight. But the sky was moonless, the sea calm and quiet.

It was April 1912. Some 2,340 eager passengers and crew were aboard the great ship *Titanic* when it left Southampton, England, for its maiden voyage to New York City. The guest list included some of the world's richest and most influential people.

The watchman called out, "Ice ahead."

The crewman at the helm immediately gave the order for the great ship to turn aside, barely missing a head-on collision with the iceberg. Ironically, although a head-on collision would have caused significant damage and perhaps injury, it probably would not have resulted in the sinking of the steamer. But when the ship turned, it allowed the massive iceberg to tear into compartment after compartment along the side of that great vessel, opening such a hole that there was no hope of saving it. Filling with water, the *Titanic* began to slowly list to one side and then to pitch ever forward into the sea.

When it became known that there were not enough lifeboats for all, many of the passengers responded heroically by helping others and refusing to go themselves. Women and children were loaded first, but many of the wives refused to leave their husbands. They stayed on board. And when all the boats were gone, when it was clear that those who were left would not survive, those valiant passengers held each other's hands and sang hymns of faith as the great ship slipped into its cold, watery grave.

The intrigue of this great disaster has not diminished with the passing of time. Scores of books and articles about it continue to be written year after year. In 1985 the remains of the *Titanic* were found resting peacefully on the ocean floor. Shortly thereafter a four-part television series about the sinking of the ship drew huge ratings coast to coast. Audiences continue to flock to the Broadway musical called *Titanic,* and the movie with that same name proved to be one of the most popular films of all time.

What is it about this event that continues to capture our imagination? Some suggest that the sinking of the *Titanic* marked the end of an era. Sociologists and historians document that the disaster had a profound effect upon society, and in many ways it became a kind of sad symbol of the early part of the 20th century. With her sank the smug Victorian dream that every day in every way, humanity was getting better and better. The disaster seemed to usher in the spirit of our present age—the Age of Anxiety.

Leaders must be constantly aware of what is happening within and around their organizations.

Some saw this catastrophe as a condemnation of the arrogance of the emerging industrial society. Because of the design of its watertight compartments, the *Titanic* was hailed widely as the ship that could never sink—and down it went on its very first voyage, taking with it the vanity of those who built her. The owners of the ship, you see, were so sure it could never sink that they did not supply the *Titanic* with nearly enough lifeboats. Why go to such an unnecessary expense?

Others saw the disaster in terms of the evils of excess. Here were these wealthy merchants and business tycoons on an extravagant voyage, and in the end they paid a great price for such luxury and privilege.

Regardless of the sociological observations of the *Titanic,* the story demonstrates the challenge of leadership when weather changes and storms threaten. Leaders must be constantly aware of what is happening within and around their organizations. They know that tough times are simply part of the cycle of organizational life.

Jesus continually prepared His followers for the tough times. He repeatedly warned them that trials would come. And sure enough they did, but the Church did not fold under the pressure; it triumphed. So, too, leaders must be able to anticipate, recognize, and survive the various "weather" patterns in the life of any organization.

Creating Positive Weather Patterns Within an Organization

Weather involves temperature, precipitation, atmospheric pressure, winds, storms, and visibility. Of all of these elements, the two most important are temperature and precipitation. If you could control these elements in the natural order, you could rule the world. Just so, if one can control these elements in the life of an organization, you can lead.

Temperature: The sun is the most important source of heat for the earth's atmosphere. Just so, the leader controls, at least in part, the temperature of an organization by bringing energy and "raising the temperature." Part of this comes from one's own energy and passion applied to leadership, but it is also accomplished by simply adding fuel to the fire already present in an organization and in the heart and life of a believer.

On one occasion Paul wrote to encourage Timothy, a young leader in the Early Church, saying, "For this reason I remind you to fan into flame the gift of God, which is in you" (2 Tim. 1:6). Fan into flame the gift of God. That is a challenge for all leaders.

Tucked away in Lev. 6:8-13 is a series of instructions given to the priests (the leaders) of Israel. The children of Israel are just becoming a nation and are just beginning their formal worship of the Lord.

> The LORD said to Moses: "Give Aaron and his sons this command: 'These are the regulations for the burnt offering: The burnt offering is to remain on the altar hearth

throughout the night, till morning, and the fire must be kept burning on the altar. The priest shall then put on his linen clothes, with linen undergarments next to his body, and shall remove the ashes of the burnt offering that the fire has consumed on the altar and place them beside the altar. Then he is to take off these clothes and put on others, and carry the ashes outside the camp to a place that is ceremonially clean. The fire on the altar must be kept burning; it must not go out. Every morning the priest is to add firewood and arrange the burnt offering on the fire and burn the fat of the fellowship offerings on it. The fire must be kept burning on the altar continuously; it must not go out.'"

Herein is a repeated call to the priests to keep the fire from going out. Other duties might be deferred, some things might be left undone—but the fire on the altar was not to go out.

You don't have to be a Boy Scout to know that a fire, if it is left untended, will indeed eventually go out. The fire on the altar in Lev. 6 was from God, but two important things had to be done in order to keep the fire burning.

<hr />

Leaders can also raise the temperature
and productivity of an organization
by removing the ashes so that
fresh air can fan the flame.

<hr />

1. *The leaders had to remove the debris—they carried the ashes away, kept the fire fresh.* If leaders are to raise the temperature, they must shake off the ashes and clear away the debris that can

accumulate and smother or at least obscure goals, methods, and even people.

When we lived in Dallas, Jill and I were visiting my parents in Ohio at Christmastime. Coming from the South, we were anxious to enjoy the fireplace at my parents' home. The day after we arrived, I noticed that the fireplace was filled with ashes, so I decided to clean it out so that we might be able to build a fire that evening.

Fortunately it was trash day. So with a small hand shovel I filled two large grocery sacks with the ashes, carried them to the curb, and put them with the rest of the trash. A few minutes later the telephone rang, and one of the neighbors said to my mother, "Your mailbox is on fire."

I ran out to the curb and quickly extinguished the flames. Evidently, buried within those ashes were yet some live embers. After putting the fire out and again containing the ashes, I returned to the house. Within minutes the same neighbor phoned once more, saying, "Your mailbox is on fire again."

By this time, most of the neighborhood was watching as I repeated the extinguishing process. This time I carried the ashes to the back of the house and poured water on them. I'd had the right idea; I just hadn't been careful enough. When the wind removed some of the ashes, the coals, buried deep, came to flame again. Leaders can also raise the temperature and productivity of an organization by removing the ashes so that fresh air can fan the flame.

2. *The leaders of Israel also took care to add new wood, to refuel.* Not only can organizational life suffer from clutter, but also it can simply burn itself out unless it is refueled. Fuel comes in many forms: capital, technology, new markets and products, new ideas and structures. Leaders will take care to raise the temperature of an organization by adding fuel.

A man was restless and dissatisfied with life. He explained his problem to a wise friend, who replied with a request. "Inhale as deeply as you can." The man did. "Now exhale as fully as you can." The man complied. The friend then said, "Now exhale again." The man tried but quickly sputtered. There comes a moment when we cannot give out any longer without taking in.

Precipitation: The leader as meteorologist also suggests that one must be aware that any organization will also need times of precipitation. It is a mistake to think of rain as a negative force. Rain refreshes the atmosphere and the earth beneath it. It is part of the cycle of moisture that includes evaporation and condensation. Leaders should realize that in the atmosphere of their organizations there is an ongoing process of evaporation. People, materials, and ideas are constantly in use, and unless these are replenished from a reservoir or "shower," the organization will diminish.

Effective leaders find ways to refresh and renew the people, materials, and mental capital of an organization. This can be done through providing time away from the job for employees (days off and vacation time), special times of training and retreat, office or organizational celebrations, ceremonies and times of recognition and incentive, enhancement of resources through added technology and/or equipment, and new employees who bring fresh ideas and perspectives with them.

The German philosopher Goethe wrote:

I have come to the frightening conclusion
that I am the decisive element.
It is my personal approach that creates the climate.
It is my daily mood that makes the weather.
I possess tremendous power to make life miserable or joyous.

I can be a tool of torture
or an instrument of inspiration.

I can humiliate or humor, hurt or heal.
In all situations, it is my response that decides
whether a crisis will be exalted or de-escalated,
and a person humanized or dehumanized.

If we treat people as they are, we make them worse.
If we treat people as they ought to be,
we help them become what they are capable of becoming.[1]

A leader is one who sees more than others see,
who sees farther than others see, and who sees before others do.
—Leroy Eims

You broaden the path beneath me, so that my ankles do not turn.
—Ps. 18:36

19

GRACE-*full* LEADERS . . .
anticipate through planning, pathfinding,
planting, and prospecting

Good leaders create positive energy that helps people overcome obstacles, break free from inertia, and rise to new challenges and levels of performance. They act in the present with the future in mind—they anticipate. This is done through planning, pathfinding, planting, and prospecting.

1. Planning: *the development of a scheme or method of proceeding*

Planning is both a process and a product. It is a detailed and usually documented way of looking at the future. The process of planning is a vital step, for it forces an organization to evaluate its mission, assumptions, expectation, and resources. Planning brings energy and signals organizational health and vitality. It is the plan that sets the course to turn good intentions into results.

A plan brings focus to energies and activities. It is amazing how many organizations do not use a master plan to chart their way. Too often leaders and managers are so preoccupied with immediate issues that they lose sight of what needs to be done now to ensure future health and vitality. Without a plan, an organization or individual simply reacts to circumstances.

It is not a question of planning or not planning, because not planning is still a plan of sorts. Planning should not be understood as an organizational straitjacket designed to restrict movement and flexibility. Having a plan is essentially an attempt to decide in advance what you will do or not do in the future. If plans are considered fixed, rigid, or unchangeable, they will often fail. Planning is dynamic. It makes room for change. In fact, it often initiates change. Reevaluation and further planning is part of every step in implementing a plan.

For the grace-full leader, planning asks whether you'll affect the future at random or with purpose and clear direction.

A sound plan serves as a framework for decisions. It assists an organization to benchmark and monitor progress and often becomes a catalyst for change and renewal within the life of an organization. Plans serve as communication tools that clarify objectives, methods, and expectations throughout the organization.

There are seven key areas in which every leader must function effectively. For planning to be adequate, it must address these functional areas of administration. To ignore one or more of these is to have an incomplete and flawed plan.

Mission—the clear, written statement of why an organization exists and what it seeks to accomplish.

Objectives—the specific targets to be achieved in order to fulfill one's mission.

Organization—the orderly arrangement of functions, resources, and personnel to meet the objectives.

Human Resources—the people and people skills needed to meet the requirements of the organization.

Physical Resources—the nonhuman, nonfinancial resources (buildings/equipment/technology) necessary to support the work of the organization.

Financial Resources—the money and financial systems to manage the money needed to fund the organization.

Controls—the systems (audits, inventories, evaluations, reviews) necessary to ensure compliance and measure progress and success.

Grace-full leaders recognize that planning is part of God's pattern. A meaningful and comforting passage of Scripture is the declaration of God found in Jer. 29:11: "'I know the plans I have for you,' declares the LORD, 'plans to prosper you and not to harm you, plans to give you hope and a future.'" God plans.

2. Pathfinding: *finding a way through the wilderness*

There is no paved road to tomorrow, no freeway to the future. There is only wilderness—a route filled with uncertain terrain, unpredictable obstacles. There are no maps and only a few random signposts along the way. So leaders must make a way, a path, and lay out a course of action.

Grace-full leaders see possibilities where others may not. They understand that often the most significant accomplishments of an organization come from exploiting opportunities, not just solving problems.

By definition leaders ought to be pioneers—people who are willing to step out into the unknown. Experimentation, innovation, and change all involve risk and adventure; yet often in striking out to find a way when and where the way is obscured, new ideas and methods are discovered. Richard Carlton, former CEO of the 3M Corporation, commented on how his company had stumbled onto some of its new products. "But never forget that you can only stumble if you're moving."[1]

The use of friendly greeters at Wal-Mart stores is an example of pathfinding leadership. Having greeters on hand to welcome folks to the store was not a strategic decision made at the corporate offices of Wal-Mart. It happened as a single store manager was searching for a way to help reduce shoplifting.

The manager decided that he would position an employee at the entrance to watch as people came in and out of the store. In addition to keeping an eye out for shoplifters, the employee began to greet the customers, offer assistance, learn their names, and establish some personal rapport with the customers. It proved to be so popular that other stores adopted the practice, and finally it became standard procedure for the company.

❦

> *One thing to remember when*
> *striking out on an uncharted course*
> *is to take along a compass.*

❦

A. J. Cronin observed: "Life is no straight and easy corridor along which we travel free and unhampered, but a maze of passages, through which we must seek our way, lost and confused, now and again checked in a blind alley. But always, if we have faith, God will open a door for us, not perhaps one that we ourselves would ever have thought of, but one that will ultimately prove good for us."[2]

One thing to remember when striking out on an uncharted course is to take along a compass. For the leader, values and guiding principles are the compass. These always point the way.

As long as you follow those key indicators, you won't be lost or confused for long. There will be a clearing in the wilderness.

3. Planting: *to put or set forth in anticipation of growth*

Administrative planting involves sowing and cultivating new prospects, programs, and people. To be a planter calls for faith, vision, and at least a measure of sacrifice. Grace-full leaders are willing to plant, knowing that even if they do not reap the harvest, others will come behind them and benefit from the actions taken now.

❦

> *After the cycle is in place, there comes a*
> *natural rhythm of sowing and reaping.*

❦

At the front end, planting costs. It takes time, energy, and resources. Only a leader with vision and discipline sees the wisdom in planting. In my work, planting takes many forms. The most obvious form is the work universities do in the area of development. Development is a code word for fund-raising. Schools and most other not-for-profit organizations recognize the value—no, the necessity—of investing now in the cultivation of donors as a way to help ensure the future financial health and viability of the organization.

It is not unusual for a development officer to work for months or even years to secure a deferred gift from someone's estate plan. And then it may take years before the university benefits directly from that gift. But after the cycle is in place, there comes a natural rhythm of sowing and reaping. However, like any farmer, one must be patient and diligent in sowing the seed and waiting for the harvest.

Universities also plant in the form of investing in people. Many schools, like most businesses, will help pay for employee schooling and professional development. The expectation is that there will come a natural and positive return, at some point, to the university in the form of added faculty degrees and/or staff competencies.

Businesses and organizations must constantly be reinvesting (planting) in order to ensure adequate facilities and equipment. Regular maintenance, strategic facility planning, and proper investments in technology are all ways that organizations replant for the future. In contrast, organizations that get behind the deferred-maintenance curve will reap a season of hardship in days to come.

4. Prospecting: *to explore, investigate, and search for something of value*

The exercise of prospecting is filled with possibility, anticipation, hope, and promise. One day in April 1992, at 6 A.M., a young manager named Tom Tiller herded 40 manufacturing workers aboard a bus at General Electric's range-building plant at Appliance Park in Louisville, Kentucky. They headed for the annual Kitchen and Bath Show in Atlanta. They were setting out on a crucial prospecting mission.

Appliance Park, a sprawling 1,100-acre complex, had once employed more than 23,000 workers. By 1992 the company had closed several of its production lines, and employment was down to 9,000. The range line was losing $10 million a year, and the jobs of everyone on that bus were in jeopardy.

GE hadn't produced a new set of kitchen ranges in 20 years. During the bus ride, the 40 people from different departments got to know each other and became more comfortable together.

At the show in Atlanta they went through every product and decided what ideas they wanted to use. At the end of the trip, there
was a very clear sense that "we've got to do something. We've
got to do it fast." And they did.

Within 18 months, the people on that bus had spearheaded
an effort that had three new products designed, built, and deliv-
ered to the market. The plant went from a $10 million loss to a
$35 million profit in 1994.[3]

Prospecting can take many different forms, but the elements remain constant. There must be some journey, real or
imagined, that opens a new source of ideas and options. Individuals must come to believe that their future and the future of their
organization is at stake, and they must therefore discover new
ways of doing things and the resources at hand with which to do
them. Prospecting also provides a measure of drama into the often ordinary and sometimes dull life of an organization.

Grace-full leaders are not willing to be satisfied with the
status quo. They anticipate through planning, pathfinding,
planting, and prospecting.

You must live with people to know their problems,
and live with God in order to solve them.
—P. T. Forsyth

He had compassion on them, because they were harassed and helpless,
like sheep without a shepherd.
—Matt. 9:36

20

GRACE-*full* LEADERS . . .
take care

Grace-full leaders learn to take care of their organizations, themselves, and their relationship to God. Unless care is consistently given to each aspect of life, a person's leadership can be eroded.

Grace-Full Leaders Take Care of Their Organizations

Mike Campbell is one of the characters in Ernest Hemingway's *Sun Also Rises*. At one point in the story, Campbell is asked how he went bankrupt. His reply is classic. "Two ways," he said. "Gradually and then suddenly."[1] That's the pattern for organizational demise. It often happens suddenly after a longer period of slow deterioration. Leaders bear the ultimate accountability of caring for the organization. No one can do it alone, but someone must ultimately bear the responsibility.

Several years ago, an office building on the outskirts of London began to develop a series of severe structural cracks. These cracks first appeared on the upper floors of the building. No one seemed too alarmed in the beginning. The cracks were considered the result of some natural settling that occasionally occurs a few years after a building is completed. But the cracks grew greater and began to spread from floor to floor.

Builders and engineers were summoned to the site, but no one, at first, could determine the source of the problem, for everything appeared to be in order. Finally the building architect, who had retired by then, was brought back to the site for consultation. After a careful inspection he asked to be taken to the basement of the building. He then proceeded down through a series of subbasements that housed some of the mechanical systems of the building. When he reached the lowest level, he discovered the cause of the problem: one large supporting wall in that subbasement had mysteriously been removed. He reported that the cause of the problem had nothing to do with the 27th floor where the cracks had first appeared; the problem was with the foundation.

All the patching, painting, and propping up in the world won't compensate for a faulty foundation.

Immediately an investigation was launched; and it was soon determined that a worker, whose job was housed in that lower basement, had begun, years before, to take a brick or two out of the wall as he left work each day. Over time he had accumulated enough bricks to build a small garage at his house.

At first it appeared that no one would ever know, for no one ever came to the subbasement. What he didn't realize was that sooner or later, the results of a weakened foundation will always appear in some part of the building.

All the patching, painting, and propping up in the world won't compensate for a faulty foundation. That's true architecturally as well as for organizations and organizational leaders.

Leaders must vigilantly take care to monitor the life and health and vitality of their organizations. This is done through the regular and careful analysis of organizational data. Leaders must be particularly sensitive to trends and patterns that at first glance may not seem too significant, but when viewed in context, over time, may reveal organizational problems. A wise leader accepts that all organizations have problems from time to time and thus tries to recognize them early and respond confidently.

Grace-full leaders are aware that an organization is held together by shared values, beliefs, and commitments. This is what gives it fiber, integrity, and the capacity to endure cyclical hardships. Since organizations are people, the first way to care for the organization is to hire the right people—individuals who are committed to the core values of the organization. One of leadership's classic axioms is to "hire for attitude and train for skills."[2]

Grace-Full Leaders Take Care of Themselves

Leadership is a process that involves many people working toward a common vision, but at the heart of it all is a person, the leader. Unless that person cares for himself or herself, the leadership will be diminished.

*There is . . . an element of
learning when not to care.*

Taking care of yourself includes caring for your health—physically, mentally, and emotionally. This begins with reflection. My father, who built an outstanding business while often working two jobs, would say from time to time that he needed "some looking out the window" time. In the midst of a very busy and productive life, he understood the need to take some time to keep his mind clear, his thoughts focused, and his heart tender.

Eric Fromm made an interesting observation when he wrote: "Modern man thinks he loses something—time—when he does not do things quickly, yet he does not know what to do with the time he gains except to kill it."[3]

Grace-Full Leaders Take Care of Their Relationship to God

For the believer, leadership is faith in action. Grace-full leaders seek God's heart, not just His hands. When we seek His hands, we are not seeking God, but what He can do for us. We take our plans and vision to Him and simply ask that He agree and bring it to pass. This can lead to a relationship based on a series of requests or even demands. To seek God's heart is to long to know Him more intimately. That takes time and concentrated desire, but it is beautifully reciprocal because the more you care for God, the more aware you become of His care for you.

There is also an element of learning when not to care. It is not wise to let the cares of the world weigh too heavily on your shoulders. Let God be God. Learn to cast your cares upon Him, knowing that He cares for you (1 Pet. 5:7, KJV).

Not long ago the sports world reported the story of a world-class female runner who was invited to compete in a road race in Connecticut. On the morning of the race, she drove from New York City, following the directions she had been given. Somehow, though, she became lost; and, being a woman rather than a man, she stopped immediately at a gas station and asked for help.

She remembered that the race was to start in the parking lot of a shopping mall. Sure enough, the attendant knew of such a race scheduled just up the road and directed her there. When she arrived, she was relieved to see in the parking lot a group of runners warming up. There weren't as many runners as she had anticipated, and she was also a bit surprised to learn that the race was shorter than she had been told. Nonetheless, she hurried to the registration desk, got her number, and began her warm-up routine. Soon they were off. She ran the race with ease, finishing minutes ahead of the second-place runner.

Only after the race had finished—when there was no envelope containing her prize money—did she confirm that the event she had run was not the race to which she'd been invited. That race had been held several miles farther up the road in another town. *She had gone to the wrong starting line, run the wrong course, and missed her chance to win a valuable prize.*[4]

Grace-full leaders take care to run the right race in the right way, to finish the course, and to keep the faith (2 Tim. 4:7).

CONCLUSION
The Challenge of Grace-Full Leadership

A business or organization that is short on finances can increase productivity and sales or borrow money. One with a poor location can move. But an organization short on leadership has little chance of survival.

Learning to lead is a lifelong process. It doesn't happen by reading a book or taking a course or wishing it were so. We all learn to lead by leading. And learning to lead is also a part of learning to live with purpose and meaning beyond our own interests and abilities.

In the final analysis, leadership development is self-development. William Pollard notes: "In the absence of grace, there will be no reaching for potential."[1] One must lead and manage from within. "Musicians have their instruments. Engineers have their computers. Accountants have their calculators. Leaders have themselves. They are their own instruments."[2] You learn to lead by leading, but not by leading alone.

To learn leadership, an individual must learn to think and evaluate actions and results; to see the relationship between exactly what was done in a given situation (with all of its complexities inherent in any situation) and what resulted. As one observes, reflects, tries, succeeds, and fails, one learns to lead.

This inductive approach to learning, where you proceed from observations based on experience to principles and applications, is the way to learn to lead. It is like the athlete who watches game films following the contest. By observing carefully what was done and not done in a given situation, learning develops. In this method, failures are often as instructive as successes.

Leadership is a challenging way of life. Jack Welch defines an effective corporate executive as someone who can change the tires while the car's still rolling. Surely this describes effective leadership in any arena.

Welch's observation speaks to the need of effectively managing the continuing work of an organization (keeping the car moving in the right direction at the right speed), while at the same time leading and bringing renewal (changing the tires), so that the organization can continue its progress into the future. He is right that these two functions, management and leadership, must be done simultaneously.

*The world is waiting for a
new generation of leaders.*

We can and ought to learn as much as possible about the art and craft of leadership from the world around us, but let us never lose sight that there is a difference. And the difference is grace. In the closing paragraph of his book *Leadership Is an Art,* Max DePree observes: "Leadership is much more an art, a belief, a condition of the heart, than a set of things to do."[3]

The grace of God enables us to focus on spirit, not just style; covenants, not just contracts; people, not just tasks; and so on. God is at work in all of our lives, and He will bless our efforts and lead His Church. I like the way David McKenna put it: "If in the course of being leaders we must err, let us err on the side of grace. More often than not it will cost us something—a slice of power, a glitter of reputation, an edge of criticism, a pain in the pit of our stomachs, a loss of sleep, and even the lesson of failure. Yet, if we act with the fullness of grace which puts people first and the fullness of truth which gives us the assurance of being fair and doing right, we will have peace."[4]

The world is waiting for a new generation of leaders—men and women whose mission is more than profit, whose morality is not contextual, and whose very life is an expression of grace; leaders who will manage themselves, inspire others, and forge the future.

Grace-filled Christian leaders are on the right track, pursuing the right ends, and struggling with the right issues. Have we arrived? Maybe not quite yet, but we continue on our way, confident, as John put it, "From the fullness of his grace we have all received one blessing after another" (John 1:16).

NOTES

Introduction

1. David L. McKenna, *Power to Lead, Grace to Follow: Strategy for the Future of Christian Leadership* (Dallas: Word Publishing, 1989), 14.

2. James MacGregor Burns, *Leadership* (New York: Harper Torchbooks, 1978), 1-5.

3. Rhonda Abrams, *Wear Clean Underwear: Business Wisdom from Mom* (New York: Random AudioBooks, Villard Books, 1999).

Section One

Chapter 1

1. Max DePree, *Leadership Is an Art* (New York: Dell Publishing, 1989), 26-27.

2. Max DePree, *Leadership Jazz* (New York: Dell Publishing, 1992), 10.

3. Bryant S. Hinckley, *Not by Bread Alone* (Salt Lake City: Bookcraft, 1955), 25.

Chapter 2

1. DePree, *Leadership Is an Art*, 12.

2. Aleksandr Solzhenitsyn, *A World Split Apart* (New York: Harper and Row, 1978), 17-19, 39.

3. David Neidert, *The Season of Leadership* (Provo, Utah: Executive Excellence Publishing, 1999), 241.

4. Warren Bennis, *On Becoming a Leader* (Reading, Mass.: Addison-Wesley Publishing Co., 1994), 163.

5. Ibid., 195.

Chapter 3

1. Warren Bennis and Robert Townsend, *Reinventing Leadership: Strategies to Empower the Organization* (New York: William Morrow and Co., 1995), 76.

2. DePree, *Leadership Is an Art*, 11.

3. Stephen R. Covey, *Principle-Centered Leadership* (New York: Summit Books, 1990), 103.

4. Bennis and Townsend, *Reinventing Leadership*, 74.

5. Bob Brower, "An Education That Makes a Difference," *Viewpoint* (San Diego: Point Loma Nazarene University, June 1999), 3.

Chapter 4

1. Covey, *Principle-Centered Leadership,* 67.

2. John P. Kotter, *Leading Change* (Boston: Harvard Business School Press, 1996), 67.

3. James C. Collins and Jerry I. Porras, *Built to Last: Successful Habits of Visionary Companies* (New York: Harper Business, 1994, 1997), 220.

4. Ari L. Goldman, *The Search for God at Harvard* (New York: Random House, 1991), 16.

Chapter 5

1. Leonard Doohan, *Laity's Mission in the Local Church* (San Francisco: Harper and Row, 1986), 64.

2. Alan Richardson, *The Biblical Doctrine of Work* (London: World Council of Churches by SMC Press, 1952), 19.

3. Ibid., 21.

4. Ibid., 33.

5. Elton Trueblood, *Your Other Vocation* (New York: Harper and Row, 1952), 57.

6. Nelvon Ross, *Monday's Ministries—the Ministry of the Laity* (Philadelphia: Parish Life Press, 1979), 21.

7. Doohan, *Laity's Mission,* 56.

8. Robert Slocum, *Ordinary Christians in a High-Tech World* (Waco, Tex.: Word Publishing, 1986), 154-68.

9. Ibid., 155-56.

10. Ibid., 159.

11. Ibid., 162.

12. Ibid., 163.

13. Ibid., 167.

14. Ibid., 66.

15. Ibid.

Chapter 6

1. Robert J. Danzig, *The Leader Within You* (Hollywood, Fla.: Lifetime Books, Inc., 1998), 93-94.

2. Noel M. Tichy and Mary Anne Devanna, *The Transformational Leader* (New York: John Wiley and Sons, 1990), 28.

3. Warren Bennis, *Why Leaders Can't Lead* (San Francisco: Jossey-Bass Publishers, 1990), 154.

Chapter 7

1. James M. Kouzes and Barry Z. Posner, *The Leadership Challenge* (San Francisco: Jossey-Bass Publishers, 1988), 60.

2. Michael J. Gelb and Tony Buzan, *Lessons from the Art of Juggling* (New York: Harmony Books, 1994), xviii.

3. John C. Maxwell, *The 21 Irrefutable Laws of Leadership* (Nashville: Thomas Nelson Publishers, 1998), 99.

Chapter 9

1. Laurie Beth Jones, *Jesus, CEO: Using Ancient Wisdom for Visionary Leadership* (New York: Hyperion, 1995), 51.

2. Janet Lowe, *Jack Welch Speaks* (New York: John Wiley and Sons, 1998), 71.

3. Albert Edward Day, *Discipline and Discovery,* in Reuben Job and Norman Shawchuck, *A Guide to Prayer* (Nashville: Upper Room, 1983), 386.

4. Hans Kung, *The Church,* in Job and Shawchuck, *Guide to Prayer,* 88.

Chapter 10

1. DePree, *Leadership Is an Art,* 12.

2. Ibid.

3. Clyde Cook, "Learning from the Lessons of Others," in *Lessons in Leadership,* ed. Randal Roberts (Grand Rapids: Kregel Publications, 1999), 81.

4. C. William Pollard, *The Soul of the Firm* (Grand Rapids: Harper Business/Zondervan, 1996), 41.

5. Tom Chappell, *The Soul of a Business: Managing for Profit and the Common Good* (New York: Bantam Books, 1993), 60.

Section Two

Chapter 11

1. Neidert, *Season of Leadership,* 240.

2. McKenna, *Power to Lead,* 145.

3. Ken Blanchard and Michael O'Connor with Jim Ballard, *Managing by Values* (San Francisco: Berrett-Koehler Publishers, 1997), 21.

4. Peggy Noonan, "Ronald Reagan," in Robert A. Wilson, *Character Above All* (New York: Simon and Schuster, 1995), 202-3.

5. Peter Petre and Margaret E. Elliott, "Jack Welch: I Got a Raw Deal," *Fortune,* July 7, 1986, 45.

6. Bob Benson, *Laughter in the Walls* (Nashville: Impact Books, 1969), 50-51.

7. James Gordon Kingsley, *Conversations with Leaders for a New Millennium* (Liberty, Mo.: William Jewell Press, 1991), 184.

Chapter 12
1. DePree, *Leadership Jazz,* 9.

Chapter 13
1. Bennis and Townsend, *Reinventing Leadership,* 161.

2. Richard Bode, *First You Have to Row a Little Boat: Reflections on Life and Living* (New York: Warner Books, 1993), 13-14.

3. D. A. Benton, *Lions Don't Need to Roar* (New York: Warner Books, 1992), 181.

Chapter 15
1. Bennis and Townsend, *Reinventing Leadership,* 6-7.

2. Clark Kerr, *The Uses of the University* (Cambridge, Mass.: Harvard University Press, 1995), 22.

3. Stephen R. Covey, *First Things First* (New York: Simon and Schuster, 1994), 126.

4. Charles R. Swindoll, *Come Before Winter* (Portland, Oreg.: Multnomah Press, 1985), 74.

Chapter 16
1. Robert L. Dilenschnieder, *A Briefing for Leaders* (New York: Harper Business, 1992), 15.

2. Kouzes and Posner, *Leadership Challenge,* 83.

3. Warren Bennis and Burt Nanus, *Leaders: The Strategies for Taking Charge* (New York: Harper and Row, 1985), 89.

Chapter 18
1. From a plaque posted in the Wisner Hall of Nursing on the campus of Olivet Nazarene University (emphasis added).

Chapter 19
1. Collins and Porras, *Built to Last,* 140.

2. Spencer Johnson, M.D., *Who Moved My Cheese?* (New York: Penguin Books, 1998), flyleaf.

3. Noel M. Tichy, *Rapid Read Handbook,* based on *The Leadership Engine: Building Leaders at Every Level* (Dallas: EPS Solutions, 1998), 33.

Chapter 20
1. Theodore Levitt, *Thinking About Management* (New York: Free Press, 1991), 99.

2. William M. Plamondon, "Energy and Leadership," in *The Leader of the Future,* ed. Frances Hesselbein, Marshall Goldsmith, and Richard Beckhard (San Francisco: Jossey-Bass Publishers, 1996), 277.

3. B. Eugene Griessman, *Time Tactics of Very Successful People* (New York: McGraw-Hill, 1994), 200.

4. David S. Dockery, "The Great Commandment as a Paradigm for Christian Higher Education," in *The Future of Christian Higher Education,* ed. David Dockery and David Gushee (Nashville: Broadman and Holman, 1999), 15-16.

Conclusion

1. Pollard, *Soul of the Firm,* 119.

2. Kouzes and Posner, *Leadership Challenge,* 277.

3. DePree, *Leadership Is an Art,* 148.

4. McKenna, *Power to Lead,* 59.

BIBLIOGRAPHY

Abrams, Rhonda. *Wear Clean Underwear: Business Wisdom from Mom.* New York: Random AudioBooks, Villard Books, 1999.

Bennis, Warren. *On Becoming a Leader.* Reading, Mass.: Addison-Wesley Publishing Co., 1994.

———. *Why Leaders Can't Lead.* San Francisco: Jossey-Bass Publishers, 1990.

Bennis, Warren, and Burt Nanus. *Leaders: The Strategies for Taking Charge.* New York: Harper and Row, 1985.

Bennis, Warren, and Robert Townsend. *Reinventing Leadership: Strategies to Empower the Organization.* New York: William Morrow and Co., 1995.

Benson, Bob. *Laughter in the Walls.* Nashville: Impact Books, 1969.

Benton, D. A. *Lions Don't Need to Roar.* New York: Warner Books, 1992.

Blanchard, Ken, and Michael O'Connor with Jim Ballard. *Managing by Values.* San Francisco: Berrett-Koehler Publishers, 1997.

Bode, Richard. *First You Have to Row a Little Boat: Reflections on Life and Living.* New York: Warner Books, 1993.

Briner, Bob. *The Management Methods of Jesus.* Nashville: Thomas Nelson, 1996.

Brower, Bob. "An Education That Makes a Difference." *Viewpoint.* San Diego: Point Loma Nazarene University, June 1999.

Burns, James MacGregor. *Leadership.* New York: Harper Torchbooks, 1978.

Chappell, Tom. *The Soul of a Business: Managing for Profit and the Common Good.* New York: Bantam Books, 1993.

Collins, James C., and Jerry I. Porras. *Built to Last: Successful Habits of Visionary Companies.* New York: Harper Business, 1994, 1997.

Cook, Clyde. "Learning from the Lessons of Others." In *Lessons in Leadership,* ed. Randal Roberts. Grand Rapids: Kregel Publications, 1999.

Covey, Stephen R. *First Things First.* New York: Simon and Schuster, 1994.

——. *Principle-Centered Leadership.* New York: Summit Books, 1990.

Danzig, Robert J. *The Leader Within You.* Hollywood, Fla.: Lifetime Books, Inc., 1998.

DePree, Max. *Leadership Is an Art.* New York: Dell Publishing, 1989.

——. *Leadership Jazz.* New York: Dell Publishing, 1992.

Dilenschnieder, Robert L. *A Briefing for Leaders.* New York: Harper Business, 1992.

Dockery, David S. "The Great Commandment as a Paradigm for Christian Higher Education." In *The Future of Christian Higher Education,* ed. David Dockery and David Gushee. Nashville: Broadman and Holman, 1999.

Doohan, Leonard. *Laity's Mission in the Local Church.* San Francisco: Harper and Row, 1986.

Drucker, Peter F. *Managing for the Future.* New York: Truman Talley Books, 1992.

Galloway, Dale, comp. *Leading with Vision.* Kansas City: Beacon Hill Press of Kansas City, 1999.

Gelb, Michael J., and Tony Buzan. *Lessons from the Art of Juggling.* New York: Harmony Books, 1994.

Goldman, Ari L. *The Search for God at Harvard.* New York: Random House, 1991.

Griessman, B. Eugene. *Time Tactics of Very Successful People.* New York: McGraw-Hill, 1994.

Hinckley, Bryant S. *Not by Bread Alone.* Salt Lake City: Bookcraft, 1955.

Job, Reuben, and Norman Shawchuck. *A Guide to Prayer.* Nashville: Upper Room, 1983.

Johnson, Spencer, M.D. *Who Moved My Cheese?* New York: Penguin Books, 1998.

Jones, Laurie Beth. *Jesus, CEO: Using Ancient Wisdom for Visionary Leadership.* New York: Hyperion, 1995.

Kerr, Clark. *The Uses of the University.* Cambridge, Mass.: Harvard University Press, 1995.

Kingsley, James Gordon. *Conversations with Leaders for a New Millennium.* Liberty, Mo.: William Jewell Press, 1991.

Kotter, John P. *Leading Change.* Boston: Harvard Business School Press, 1996.

Kouzes, James M., and Barry Z. Posner. *The Leadership Challenge.* San Francisco: Jossey-Bass Publishers, 1988.

Levitt, Theodore. *Thinking About Management.* New York: Free Press, 1991.

Lowe, Janet. *Jack Welch Speaks.* New York: John Wiley and Sons, 1998.

Maxwell, John C. *The 21 Irrefutable Laws of Leadership.* Nashville: Thomas Nelson Publishers, 1998.

McKenna, David L. *Power to Lead, Grace to Follow: Strategy for the Future of Christian Leadership.* Dallas: Word Publishing, 1989.

Morris, Tom. *True Success: A New Philosophy of Excellence.* New York: Berkley Publishing Group, 1994.

Neidert, David. *The Season of Leadership.* Provo, Utah: Executive Excellence Publishing, 1999.

Noonan, Peggy. "Ronald Reagan." In *Character Above All.* New York: Simon and Schuster, 1995.

Pearce, Terry. *Leading Out Loud.* San Francisco: Jossey-Bass Publishers, 1995.

Petre, Peter, and Margaret E. Elliott. "Jack Welch: I Got a Raw Deal." *Fortune,* July 7, 1986, 45.

Plamondon, William M. "Energy and Leadership." In *The Leader of the Future: New Essays by World-Class Leaders and Thinkers,* ed. Frances Hesselbein, Marshall Goldsmith, and Richard Beckhard. San Francisco: Jossey-Bass Publishers, 1996.

Pollard, C. William. *The Soul of the Firm.* Grand Rapids: Harper Business/Zondervan, 1996.

Richardson, Alan. *The Biblical Doctrine of Work.* London: World Council of Churches by SMC Press, 1952.

Roberts, Wes. *Leadership Secrets of Attila the Hun.* New York: Warner Books, 1985.

Rosovsky, Henry. *The University: An Owner's Manual.* New York: W. W. Norton and Co., 1990.

Ross, Nelvon. *Monday's Ministries—the Ministry of the Laity.* Philadelphia: Parish Life Press, 1979.

Senge, Peter M. *The Fifth Discipline.* New York: Doubleday, 1990.

Slocum, Robert. *Ordinary Christians in a High-Tech World.* Waco, Tex.: Word Publishing, 1986.

Smith, Richard Norton. *The Harvard Century: The Making of a University.* New York: Simon and Schuster, 1986.

Solzhenitsyn, Aleksandr. *A World Split Apart.* New York: Harper and Row, 1978.

Swindoll, Charles R. *Come Before Winter.* Portland, Oreg.: Multnomah Press, 1985.

Thrall, Bill, Bruce McNicol, and Ken McElrath. *The Ascent of a Leader.* San Francisco: Jossey-Bass Publishers, 1999.

Tichy, Noel M. *Rapid Read Handbook,* based on *The Leadership Engine: Building Leaders at Every Level.* Dallas: EPS Solutions, 1998.

Tichy, Noel M., and Mary Anne Devanna. *The Transformational Leader.* New York: John Wiley and Sons, 1990.

Trueblood, Elton. *Your Other Vocation.* New York: Harper and Row, 1952.

ADDITIONAL LEADERSHIP BOOKS FROM BEACON HILL PRESS

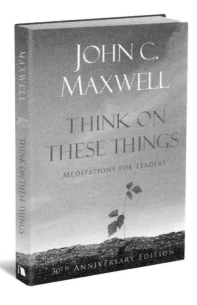

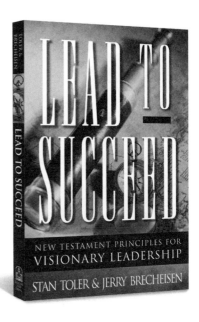

Through the power of the Spirit, the leaders of the Early Church brought Christianity from obscurity to greatness. *Lead to Succeed* will teach you the leadership secrets of these thoroughly dedicated men and women, from John the Baptist to John the Revelator.

978-0-8341-1980-2

Think on These Things contains meditations that will challenge you to reach your full potential as a leader and servant of God.

978-0-8341-2500-1

LOOK FOR THEM WHEREVER CHRISTIAN BOOKS ARE SOLD!

BEACON HILL PRESS
OF KANSAS CITY